Speak, Speak

Poetry by Gene Hirsch

edited by Judith R. Robinson

INTRODUCTION: SPEAK, SPEAK

Dr. Eugene Hirsch, Gene, to all who know him, has extended to me the priviledge of editing his poetry, an assignment I accepted with pleasure.

This collection, "Speak, Speak," is the culmination of Gene's long career of writing, and reflects the complexity of his mind and experience. As a physician/writer he joins a distinguished list, and in my opinion as a reader/editor, he earns his place among the others, notably Maugham, Chekov, William Carlos Williams.

As for the writing itself, there are several major threads, the first being a poetry that reflects a clear connection with music. As a young child, Gene was considered a musical prodigy. He played and composed for the piano under the tuteledge of Stefan Wolpe. His word for the confluence of music and words in his work is *inflection*. This is not only a matter of similarities, he says. Rather, the music connects with the poetry to produce very specific emotional resonances.

Imagination also plays a significant role in his poetry, as does his interest in mysticism and mythology. In "Maria Sabina," the poem that won the 2019 Westoreland Literary Award, he writes of the woman's death:

When Maria Sabina died,/someone twisted the neck / of a rooster and laid it by her side. On the fourth/day, not the third or the fifth,/ its spirit rose up and crowed,/calling her soul to depart, / to start its journey/ to the Dead Land,/ feeding on squash seeds, /greens and fruit along the way.

Another influence has been his broad education both in medicine and the arts. As a physician there has been the constant preoccupation with life itself, especially the matters of meaning and mortality. The most basic questions are dealt with; the answers are offered with humility. The interpretations of other artists are considered and interpreted as well. As a result of Gene's interest in their work we have answers to big questions from the likes of Byron, Beethoven, Bach, Fellini, Dali, Goya, Handel, Red Grooms and others.

Finally, "Speak, Speak," is a collection of two hundred and eighty two poems that reflects a long life remarkably well-lived. This is a book filled with people, places and world events, interpreted by a keen and curious observer.

Thank you, Gene!

JRR/6/2020

Contents

Speak

Delusional guilt, gilded garbage!
Complexity is an outlook,
sophistication, brocade.

I ask my dog to

SPEAK! SPEAK!

He only barks
and I'm disappointed.

My cat has not smiled for generations.

My friends gird their rage,
pound and pestle each other
with constant injunctions.

Kindnesses turn to pious gloss.
Tongues abound.
Doubts die soon
in looms of evasion.

We take maxims for coverlets
while sacred books must rust
in sallow fields of derision.

Poor books!
Poor no-more-talking books,
lost from the grist of their verses.

In the hearts of our minds
we shun the sterile din
of our watchword,

SPEAK!

We hide in shuffles of silence.
We live on magic and myth. .
In the end, the Gorgons come
to eat us.

Going Down to Sleep

(moderato)
Deep in the going down to sleep
lies a murmur in your licorice voice,
with a frequent cackle and laugh
in your trolley, racing round
from one to another-other,
from here-to-here,
making such a thing of it all.

How can I tell when laughter
turns to fright? Men and dogs
both snarl and bite
but as angels, must be cuddled.

Snarl now? Nooooooo.
Only at growling time
or you flush down the spout.

Wait, wait. *Attentez, mon cher.*
Waiting..........., waiting.............,

Now!
Snarl-snarl, bite-bite,
my little friend. Sing along.
Mon cher ami, chante avec moi,
Répétez. Répétez .

Growling time! Growling time!

(andante)
Year after year, I follow my trolls
who pray to the moon.
Their devotions, du jour et nuit,
each day and night, encircle me.

By now, I am weary am I
of such seductive illogic:

Follow year trolls,
snarl pray jour et nuit,

while angels lie scrunched,
bunched out of town,
aghast in a ditch by the roadside
incessantly mumbling, Répétez. Répétez...

We all eat oat-meat-bungle with a slice of slauce,
bite a rubber bone, chase a rubber mouse-toy.
We stuff them in our tucker bags.
It's cold outside. We cuddle.

(allegro con brio)
On-time, trolley! Frequent, racy.
The conductor sweeps up the aisle,
Where's your ticket, dog,
Where's your ticket, cat,
Where's your ticket, mouse,
Where's your ticket, troll,
Take-a-ticket, angel.

And here we come,
round the corner, ho-hi-ho,

singing our ding-dong-ding,
and off. Everyone off and out.
Same stop—new town,
racing round the merry-go-go.

(dolcemente con orgoglio)
Play Frequent Trolley with a SHOUT,
with a cackle and a runcible SNARL.
Laugh in your liquorish voice,
meow and mumble, then hurry to GO
in contortions of words and strange phrases.

Take your nightmares in from the cold.
Fold them in your tucker bag.
Sweep your ins and outs from one to another-other.
Ride yourself down to sleep and up the street!

Follow me faintly with your strutting-glance,
with your snicker, as I stroke you
gently from here-to-here, from ear-to-ear,
with lumps of succulent stars.

Mirra, Mirra on the Wall

For the love of shoes,
long sloping roller coaster pumps
with six foot stilettos,
giant feet of a woman—
the shoe-mobile rides again,
chauffeured by the fashionable lady,
angry, perched between its pointed toes.
A cocky sport with a fat cigar
reclines on the slope of the insole,
flapping the air with flicks of ash,
snot and snide remarks.

Holly sprouts in a tall red boot,
greets the woman
at a traffic light, whispering,

Wreck the car and ditch the sport.
She reigns her red pump to a halt,
packs herself up,
slips a foot into the tall red boot,
sprouts holly, limps home.

Contrary to what you might think,
the fat wanking sport understands.

Painted Floor

Paint the floor with faces.
Scour their teeth.
Stroke their foreheads.
Powder their cheeks.
Search for thoughts in their eyes.

Your paintbrush sweeps
through a concert of smiles
in tones that wind back
like flowing hair
dissolved in the crotch of a morning.
Arms and feet of flutes and violins
waltz across the sticky floor.
Flugel-horns blurt Baroque.
Cellists display their bounding joy.

Choirs sigh and blur,
"Sleep ye on a walls. Watch
ye selves on the brand wet floor."
Rhythms are a byte away,
glissandos smooth and tasty.

Perceptions

Each key of the piano
has a different tale to tell
in a different voice.
Dark glasses keep out
the truths of after-tones.
Hammers
beat sickles into bullets
packed in orange crates of Wheaties,
champions for breakfast.
Ho Mao, on toast with a goblet
of toadies and a stupor of juice.
Teeth walk around in fine suits
chomping on the news of the day.

Lunch With Mary

Today I am feeling my way to salvation.
My cleansing thoughts help.
Yes, indexed in this little book,
I pull *myself* out each time I wander.
I think *myself* through,
then re-index my mind
on a new page that best suits
the spiritual state I've attained.

Sometimes I share myself
with others like you,
with a cleansing thought or two, here,
in a window seat
in this ostentatious soup kitchen,
if you please. So serene,
such *Re-creative Reveries*
(as I sometimes call them)!

My fingers travel faster and faster.
The pedals seem to wander
farther and farther from
the balls of my feet.
I wrap my left toes around the lyre
to hold me from drifting back
from the keyboard. The piano plays on.

The music drains my hands,
chisels the crowd
that fills the great hall,

knowing there is no return. None.
I cannot stop, only ease back
and watch my fingers guide us all
through that awesome fugue,
after which I am obliged
to graciously fawn
and bow to the crowd.

I spend my evenings lying in bed
with the sheer luster of my sheets,
twisting and turning
to find a state of mind
in which to sleep.

My thoughts are stifled,
crowded into boxes,
my feelings, into balls of yarn,
my nightly walk to the gallows,
submerged in a tank of confusion
protests the coming of dawn,
when I'll wake to a mood
in which I'll find
my most sublime contempt
for the delusions
that make my psyche happy.

They want to convict me
for my brash
in a jail where the inmates
play games of scorn and derision;
walls plastered with nudities,
bars, spider webs
stronger than steel,

woven by the paws
of six-legged creatures
who trap their prey
and suck them dry
before they go to sleep—

Each morning,
I feel my way to redemption.
Yes, with this small notebook,
I find *myself* meandering.
I think of my elegance
then re-index myself on a new page
that best suits the holy state
which I strive to attain.

Sleep

I move slowly
from one moment to the next,
as if creeping over a desert,
searching for a verdant limb
to sprout from the trunk
of a decimate tree.

I see the wrinkled face of a clock
folded over a bough.
I reach for its days and nights,
for its months, years,
for its calloused hands,
shackled, struggling to be free.

I try to sleep but am shaken
over again by carrion crows,
by clones of chattering vultures
that gnaw at my body,
rushing to capture my spirit
as well.

I try to dream of heroes and their courage,
but can only pretend.

Dybbuk

Rage flows down her face,
tinted with greed,
with a cunning smile.
she bursts into fits and flames.

Her eyebrows stretch to squinting sticks.
Her hair lags, braided webs
of singed black stalks.

Fetor lives in her armpits,
in the folds of her groin,
like vermin, silently thriving.

She wears a winter shade of gray,
clutching her keepsakes,
her broken teeth, broken amulet,
with a grim glint of dark.

If I told you she was my wife,
If I told you I lie with her in bed—
But she's not.

She's but a shadow of my wife
in the form of a naked hag
who takes whatever you give her,
then grabs much more.

I've assuaged her hunger,
fed her with tears,
measured my pain by her anger.

I sometimes wrap myself
around the nape of her neck at night,
make love in the thicket of sleep,
then cry.

Black Tea

Have you ever lived in a house
with a roof that reached
to the outer limits of the sky?

A room with paper walls
and a shaded lamp
that hung from the heavens,
shredding light in all directions—
apparitions, confusion
in your dismal state of mind?

Have you never drawn pictures
of your wilderness, passages,
mazes on your walls,
using crayons that melted
from the warmth of your hand,
from delight in your caches of memory?

Would you have found your pictures soothing?
Might you have thought you'd created
a cloister for all time?

Could you not have soon come to feel pervaded,
engulfed, distressed, oppressed, pained,
seized, suffering from absurdity?

Could you have tried to measure your absurdity,
two spoonsful in a sludge of black tea?

Young Woman on Horseback

Sleep breathes. Evening eats
from my hand a flaming orange-
spinach salad.

Easter loves the lilies that wilt
on the porch, aching,
three full blooms by April noon.

Soon your smile will blur,
shifting itself from side to side.

Ice floes will melt, boulders split,
shale will drop from tangled slopes.

Dandelions will fly across the thicket,
across the sundown. in the morning breeze.

Today swings open wide.
It lives among us, shouts once more
and again:

Ride on, my love,
            across the meadow.
Ride swiftly on.

In the Shop Window

Combed by apples and grapes,
champagne candlesticks on a pile
of last night's feast of quartered grouse
and silver lobster leftovers soaked in ice
that never melts, with a mantle clock,
alive with ticks and tocks of staves
that rouse me from dispassion,
enticing, beckoning—

To what purpose?
Where does it lead?

Sepia talkies leap off the screen.
I pay myself the price of admission
and view me again and again
with my mannequin, Sylvia,
more frequently, more fervently
than I would care to admit;
all things considered, more devoutly
than I would ever let you know.

Loft

We came together
in the abandoned loft.
My excitement rose
to be with someone
I could trust.

As we spoke,
she opened her sack.
She offered me a wig.
As we chatted,
she offered me a silken dress.
We quipped
as she painted my lips,
tinted my cheeks,
primped my hair.

I fell into her stockings
and shoes. She gasped
to see me rise, strut and gaze
in her mirror, curtsy and smile,
and bend to kiss her forehead.

I captured her exuberance
from the corner of my eye,
just as she opened her arms
to engulf the evening,
just as she gathered herself
with the passion of seeing me
happy again.

Two Dimensions

I

A blue gentleman takes off his cap
and coat
in a forest of gangly women

with mirrors that hang
from scalloped columns
and trees. Pears and peaches fill a bowl
          on the table.
The trees turn square. Columns grow in stature.
A two dimensional naked maiden appears
          from behind a pillar to ask the blue gentleman,
a postman, you see,
to please put on his pants
and jacket and hat.
He obliges in the forest near the sea. The women frolic
with each other.
Pestilence gone, the postman grows a beard.

Only he and pears remain
          untouched in the round wooden bowl on the table.

II *

Circa 1501, In the midst of a luxuriant landscape,
a surgeon removed an object
from the forehead of a fool

who was tied to a chair. Instead of a stone,
a tulip appeared.
A second tulip lay on the table.
A book perched itself on the head of a rector.
    The monk came to bathe
in his fountain of youth. Both claimed wisdom.
But, oh, Holy, Holy. They caroused with the peasants
on a nearby boat,
an enormous casket with a blooming tree
for a mast and twigs for rudders. Small skulls munched
refuse on deck.
The fool was strung to the rigging that day.
Sooner or later, they must all suffer.
They must be forgiven.
Meanwhile, what can be said to ease the pain?

          * from The Ship of Fools (circa 1501)
          Heronimus Bosch
          Paris, Musee National du Louvre

Thank You Very Much

Bedtime lays my mortality to rest,
washes it down to where
it can no longer be tasted,
onto a planet where giants boast,
where fairy queens
wear tightly woven muslin gowns
and wield their wands—
time to sleep, pull up the blankets
and goodnight—if you please,
thank you very much.

Pasty ghosts, more and more abundant,
        float through the windows and doors.
They drape themselves as portraits
on the walls and grimace.
They quibble over lofty plans
for my sojourn to eternity.

But morning passes through the house.
Galaxies came and galaxies gone,
born and died along the road to school,
where I've learned to curtsy,

good day
and *thank you very much,*
if you please.

The Wind and I

I saw the wind. He was beautiful.
I walked through a desert
in the golden heart of the sun.

The desert turned glacial green.
The wind and I made love on a knoll.

We curled into currents and drifts.
He watched me turn through the chapters
of my childhood, purple spots
and sumptuous smells.

Today, I pack his flowers, bushes, and trees
into the pockets of my dress,
gazing in my mirror to watch him sleep,
to hear his voice, to touch him by my side.

Am I supposed to know
why clouds, like children,
fly home and rain and go to bed?
Why children drench themselves
in clouds before they sleep?
Am I supposed to know?

They never helped me understand
my flights through the songs
of the handsome wind.
They never helped me ride
the currents that sweep
through the life I live tonight.

In the Season of the Golden Goat

after the art of Francisco Goya*

Timeliness is in vogue,
bought in the market
at a price too dear
while modesty slips
through a hole
in a pocket of a monarch,
crushed even smaller
under foot.

Novelty burns in every wind.
As winds burn awhile,
differences dote on oats
and berries, rusted cream.
Quests bear quests,
each more extreme-
ly alike, more
to dislike, more the less
with shams of meaning,
more and more
their likes demeaning.

Avarice blooms on the every-stage,
studding steeds, feting fallow.
Cleats and claques
and puppets follow
with their suave, durable,
regal effluvium.

Henchmen,
catarrhal howls,
cheer for the haughty
who, bloating their bowels,
exhibit their novelty,
avarice, timelessly bartered,
bedraggled and bought.

In the swirling season of the Golden Goat,
garlands on his horns, goshawks in his heart,
he holds his court at the zenith of a crescent moon.

Pompous shadows dance to their deaths,
prancing, bungling, ratcheting spells,
chanting cadenzas for wild brazen witches
who cackle and shriek:

Together we gather to steal a fat hog,
home again, home again, jiggity jargon.
  And dress him and stuff him and baste him with glee,
          with sacrificed children, with bones and with ashes,
lovingly sprinkled with citrus and cloven
debris,
with bleating and beating and bleeding
  and bloating..........

My Scrofulous queen,
rector of witches and jowls,
steps from her crotch
in festoons of splendor.
Charmed by the strains
in her whinnies, she struts

through the cold-hearted
eyes of Madrid.

In the Year of our Lord,
at the height of the Sabbath,
in the swirling season
of the Golden Goat,
garlands on his horns,
goshawks in his heart,
she genitally fingers
her feathers and froth,
wisped and whisked,
washed and dressed,
crawling through frenzies
of tangled decrees,
midst clanging of cymbals,
past bands and bandannas,
and blabber, bravado,

Together we gather to kill our great god,
home again, home again, jiggity jargon.
And dress him and stuff him
and baste him with glee,
with sacrificed Hebrews,
with bones and with ashes,
with kings and their totems
sprinkled with citrus and cloven.

Reference: In the Season of the Golden Goat

Inspired by socially poignant masterworks
of Francisco Goya (1746-1828)

Scene of Witchcraft (1798)
(Museo de la Fundacion Lazaro Galdiano, Madrid)

Burial of the Sardine (?1800) - festivity of Death
(Museo de la Academia de Bellas Artes
de San Fernando, Madrid)

The Old Women: Until Death (ante 1812) –
doddering pretensions
(Musee des Beaux-Arts, Lille)

Procession of the flagellants (?1800) -
the Inquisition
(Museo de la Academia de Bellas Artes
de San Fernando, Madrid)

Dead and Alive

from a Japanese butoh dance

Three slivers of light
drop from the ceiling.
They follow the nude shadows
of three castrate bodies,
cowering, tangled
in pools of self-effacement,
silently nibbling their way
across the stage.

Their shoulders sag.
Spines curl,
heads thrust forward,
torsos turning as on spits
over sparking embers.

Their hands reach down
to cover their crotches.
With timid steps,
they eat the empty space
across the stage.

A white-draped figure
sprawls on the scene,
hovering prone, close above the floor.

He crashes down, wringing his body
like a jealous spider,

a venomous snake, poised to strike
and slither away.

The cowering dancers swoon in awe.
They suffer. They struggle.
They lurch as they die.
The lights from above rise slowly.
The empire crumbles.
The curtain descends.
The theater breathes life.
.

To the River of the Sea

Water flows heavily down the Yangtze   .
Heavily tainted
with foreign blood.

Overflowing, it squanders the countryside,
the yoked, the Ox-Head and Horse-face,
mantles and mortars,
nimble fingers and faces of the land.

Tempests
carry home its tide to bed.
They mock my serenity.

But, Lord Thunder,
the frenzied river knows,
seeking those who abide,
sweeping all else to the sea,

to the triumph of the Watchmen of the Sea
who sift our silt in the discharge
of their duties, in homage
to redeeming faith.

Finding His Way

My friend has begun to die,
painfully shunning the call.

Spring has become the mordant
for the colors of his life,
lodged in the folds of his skin,
in the trabeculations of his heart.

Poppies, blanched white petals,
lavender tufts,
poppies, reduced to a liquor,
flux back and forth
through the worst of his pain.

Each night, his delusions glean
what his eyes cannot bear to see.

He dreams of a well
in a parched field.
He listens for the echoes
of a stone he drops
deflecting from the shale
that lines its chasm,
splashing in the pool below.

He grasps the winch,
creeps down the braided rope
to the bucket at the end,

repeats a song from childhood,
loosens his grip,
and falls unceremoniously
to the center of Earth.

Marcella

Marcella is many years
older than her self.

Her cotton stockings
clump below her knees;
her housedress wreaks
as house clothes
often swim in stains;
she bobs her body,
pumps her wheelchair
through the hall,
two strokes forward,
one stroke back,
tearful, half-blind,
streaked with grief,
moans loosely swaying
on her lips.

As sorrows lose their way,
as hours turn
groans to mutters,
sympathy wanes.

She offends our hopes,,
neither primping
nor striving for fame
nor riches
nor consummate love.

Who is Death?

Cloaked, scythe in hand,
you race your steed across a knoll
of boulders turned to bloodshed,
chaos, distemper.

I'm told you sell disguises,
trifles, urns, figurines, saints
from mountain summit cloisters
crowned with shrines, to haunted caverns,
hoarded booty, jewelry, pollen, slime,
like tinctures of milt from craven satyrs
fondling their desires on a torrid night.

Oh Death, we will meet in the thicket of our tongues,
I, a string of beads round my neck
and you, with your scalloped eye,
witness to the swagger of cynics who preach
hubris through the gulags of hell.

Death, stand up! Stand up wherever you are,
so I may tell you
the ways I wish to hold your hand.

Find me with your cunning, your pleated shirt
and proper suit, boutonniere, suave, scented,
so I may sniff you from amongst your imposters.

Soon you'll adore me, seduce me.
You'll whisper my name

and I'll whimper some of yours.
You'll burst with envy, melt my suitors,
yearn and crave.

Death, assuage my crimes. With your trumpet of lies,
convince me that my sins will not stunt my days,
that you'll claim me not by greed, but by some thread
of compassion, so I may live my wishes
without fear of Time.

Present yourself as my escort with more wisdom than I.
More worldliness. Tout me with pomp. Beseech me.

Help me to a tart, an hor d'oeuvre, a crepe,
bon-bon, canapé·, petite haute cuisine.
Offer me a cordial, a goblet, your unction.

Sound your flügel horn, I, my oboe d' amore,
spinning devotion through our merry pranks,
our bestial love, climbing to spark the aurora
with night-storms from the burgeoning sun.

Grant me my Totentanz, my Fantastique,
macabre, lento, presto, lighter, wilder,
swirling in a furious caper that urges us
ever closer to the marble staircase
that sweeps us down and out the hall,
the regal ball, to Euphoria.
To the seizures of night.

Lead me to fortune, Fortunatissima,
Feed me your soul in delectable shades

of rose petal dust.
Cleanse my wounds with maggots.
Calm my convulsions.
Soften my twitches.
Wipe the salt from my eyes.

In that instant, you'll have held me
in a climax that rises, that crests
beyond my power to imagine,
an irresistible Queen of Abundance
in love at the height of her demise.

Marie

Snowflakes swim through your eyes

your brown woven irises
senile arcs that surround your sight
crisscross ribbons
behind your lids   I watch you
caged by bed rails

milky crescents
white with
tiny veins
a fetus
fixed on my smile

I shrink   drawn back by
your futile gestures
buttocks' stinking craters

your stifled words
useless limbs
scorching pain

You turn
drowned in a
breath
that bids goodbye
through the night
between the rails

in fitful starts
shallow
voice
pleading
My fingers crawl
to touch you

on your way to the Dead-Land.

I'll speak

as if the house has asked for you
and our street is wondering where you've been.

Flocks of birds, red, azure, yellow,
have flown across my mind,
kindling in me strokes of our belonging.

Days and years will cry
to tell you their names.

And I'll find the instant you joined the flock,
crossed the fields to the last frontier.

I'll find the name of the woman
who held your hand,
who wove your handsome robe
to shield you from falling dead trees.

Canarsie

How would I know?
He calls from the crowbars,
from the swings, walks me home,
sings in the bath, not too hot,
with words I've heard the day before.

I dress. So does he. I take him for a walk
as if he were my pet.
He plays in my sandbox,
steals my gumballs, makes a mess.

We ride my bike over the sea to Spain,
to the farthest town I can see in the sky.

When I smile, he smiles. When I cry,
as I often do, he sees me squint—
wipes my forehead when I fever,
covers my chills with a blanket.

Once in a while, I rush to the toilet
to upchuck. He holds my forehead.
My face turns red.

Ghosts in my bed make me scream
and shift myself to the other side,
then shift back and scream some more.
He calms me down.

Only a swami can see into the future—
a small chunky man
with a slicked-down beard,
hands on the table in a dark room,
a large purple jewel
on his right fourth finger.
Only a swami understands.

We run away. We catch a trolley.
Three cents for me. He goes free.
We watch the motorman smirk,
smiling best he can to a small kid
on a trolley at night.

He wrenches the handle
on his throttle to check his speed,
bumping through the city to Canarsie—
Animal Hospital, Family Dentistry,
Rockaway Park, Flatlands Avenue, Remsen,
where we step down,
where a ten person Army of Saviors revs up its band.
I drop them a penny. Harvey agrees.
Uncle Loewy comes to drive me home.
Next day, I start school.

Deputy Minister of Defense

I

The wind wakes the chickens,
beheaded, running everywhere at once,
fleeing the monster-mover
that comes to shift the earth,
its corrugated shacks,
junk with piles of broken flesh and courage;
Soweto, sliced into clotted cakes of shock.

Fingers, like the claws of chickens,
scrape themselves bare,
scratching the ground.
Black bodies scamper,
flailing aimlessly here and there,
gushing pain as they flee.

Then the quiet. Not a voice. Not a word.
Until suddenly, from the muddy ground:

Death to the silence of the night!

II

In the evening shadow,
she sits on her hands,
on the muscles of her arms.
And her babies? In that ditch,

small and still.
When she calls them,
when she tells them to come home
and eat their dinner and go to bed,
they whisper, *We are small and still.*

Others whisper too.
They speak slowly and softly
for they are also dead.
Some shout that they live,
but they're not correct.
Their retching bodies
rot to headlines
in the summer stench.

III

I think you have not known me well.
My skin is black,
my organs and my mind.
And I stand here in your court
knowing you will eat me.

My travails have been to you
like empty pages in a school of cynics
and scones and tea, of rustling lives
that fall each night from the feet of your beds.

I think I've told you with my body
all the words you need to know.

Soon each bullet from each rifle
of each marksman will purse my skin
to shatter, each, its own special
part of me. Dropping slowly
through lethal space, I will lie in state,
the soles of my feet toward Soweto,
along the road, amidst the noise
and the wheezing old busses
that have carried me
back and forth through the hottest
parts of the day.

IV

A man to be murdered;
an innocent man sentenced to die
by the neck. A baby suckles in the belly
of his woman.

I hear the cast-iron wheels
of the cart that rolls to the gibbet.
I see the noose that sits on the sheen
of his broad black shoulders,
that circles his day, and the lever
that will drop his shoes, his pants,
his shirt, and the beating of his heart
through a hole in a wooden floor,
with the sudden crick of a lifeless goodbye.

I feel the chill that will sweep him away
on its engine, that will speed him along
to the land of psalms.

And I will go to the mountain to pray:
Die in peace my lovely one.
Die in peace, my child.
The sandman will smile
upon your sorrow
and I will see you soon again.

Grief can tear a brain to shreds—
burning brown boots worn thin,
cracked, sunken deep
in the weariness of their journey.

Two boots quarrel, marching together
each quicker to match the other's stride.

Feet rot violet, blanch with pain
that shrugs its way up the legs
and into the groin of a gun-made man.

In the blare, with a banner of glory,
fervor warms him for a while,
then he freezes, stiff and splintered,
raw, peeling and proud, at attention, at ease.

Where Do You Wander?

Where do you wander
in this kingdom of stone?

My visions yield deep
dipping waters of beauty.

And where do you sleep
in this stone scattered space?

In palaces, orchards,
in wheat fields,
on blankets
of mushrooms and moss.
I sleep under bridges,
in torrents and tempests,
            with showers of stars.

And where do you
follow yourself
in the morning?

I wade in the Drina
my river of rushes and sludge,
that takes me to islands
and inlets and caverns,
with herons that live in the sky
and minnows that bathe
in white wine through
the summer—

and children that laugh
on the banks of small puddles
in the heaven of mud.

The Busman

I

A small polished stone
lies on a hillside. Each day,
a dear old man comes to pray.
Heaven sheds its light upon him.

A cloud floats in the sky
and it rains. But only on him.
Only his black hat and suit
and beard get wet.

Each morning a driver
stops his bus for the children
to play. The tzadik lifts his head.
He interrupts his prayer.
He turns in wonderment
through the pouring rain
to see the radiant sunlight
on their handsome faces.

II

The busman weeps
as he ploughs
through the snow.

A kind old man
draws a nachtlied
from the throat
of his splintered violin.
Ten waxen faces
face forward,
stories stitched
to their collars,
numbers to their arms,
misery on their lips,
terror in the foliage
of each eye.

At the end of the line,
I hear from heaven
the shrill cry of a shofar
bleeding in the night.

III

In this old castle,
in the center of a Great Hall,
stands a lonely desk. Upon it
lies only a feather pen
and an open book.

Giant tapestries drape the walls
with tales of a small desk
in the center of a great hall,
a feather pen and an ancient book.

Her eyes peer out from behind
her father's black fur coat.
She sighs with a young girl's tremble,
longing more than anything else
to mount, grasp its white mane,
and race a mighty unicorn
across an empty page.

The Busman hides His smile
beneath the furrows in His face
and drives on.

The Child

When a furrow stretches down
across the folds of a forehead,
when it cuts deep and lasting
into the right hand corner of a swollen lip,
when time buries a person's fright
and silence covers pain—
that is a scar.

You may have seen her beaded eyes,
cheeks ripe with sweat.
You may have seen me
hold her close, stroke her face,
limp by the way it hung
like a mask in a smog,
by the way she cowered,
clutched my collar,
lost herself between
each word I had to say.

You saw me ask her to smile,
dry white powder pressed to chalk--—
her hands, picket fences, splintered stakes—
her strangled hair.

I reached for her fractured mind,
searched each day, each ugly night
for the grief that buried itself inside her.

I ask myself when the sun goes down,
where is the verse or song
that might help this child learn to cry?
Is there no refuge in solace?

About A Man

I've seen you struggle
in second hand novels,
every page a headstone
suffused with gangrenous etchings,
illustrations of slithering honchos
drumming their daughters in their sleep.

I've heard you moan
on second run side streets,
with scraps and ragbags,
where pitiful packs of mankind
came to swallow you nude.

You've hidden behind a porous mask,
a smiling trademark
on a filthy skin of night.

You come to me now as an epilogue,
an afterthought on a cancelled page,
an effigy tossed on a heap,

dressed in the paper gown
of a Kewpie doll with wary eyes
that blind the fetid air,
fractured arms that fuse
to the shape of a woman
who searches for kindness—
a statue of boughs and branches
forged in a forest of shale—
to grasp what is left of daylight,
my love.

Iron Syrup

Sparks rained down
from a giant vat,
through a blistering night,
tapping red hot syrup
that spilled into veins
on an open hearth;
A leather gloved,
steel-tipped shoed
tawny man, reeked sweat.

The mill succumbed
to a fog of green paper coins.

He dragged his body
through spit and spindle.

He choked on his beggary gin,
on his cough, retching.

He crashed and disappeared
from the surface of Earth.

A Piano Lies Prostrate in a Barren Field

I

A shot rings out—cellos cry,
their voices grow forced and frail.

A shot rings out, imploding the violins.
They huddle together with a shriek
heard into the hinterlands
where few have emerged from the thrust
of the steel decrees
that have torn apart the ages.
Violas hang themselves in effigy.

A piano lies prostrate in a barren field
where vivaces once graced its elegance
as far as the eye could see.

II

Romantics lie in wait
for eruptions of the heart.
They touch our eyes and ears
with their voices, their organs of love.

Rainbow streamers twirl
from rivers of promise and daring
adventures and cause.

Cause. Messenger of life.
Passions stripped
of their pants and shirts,
their blouses and skirts,
bound with mordent wishes.

A piano lies prostrate in a barren field.
A cause rings out, forced and frail,
as far as the eye can see.

There is Nothing More to Say

There is nothing more to say
than to dissect your words
into single letters
and define them by their sounds,
each smeared
across the tortured smile
on your face.

I tramp through your fields of tulips,
crushing them as if they were
helpless children on a battlefield.

I wrap you in whirlpools of diatribes,
enunciated from my forehead.
Teeth lurk in the lights of my eyes.

I toss crass thoughts
from the palm of my hand
while I cry through each
enormous instant
for you to disarm me,
depose me,

so I cannot come near enough
to hurt you again.

Old Man

Sometimes I'd follow you into the evening,
to the corner where you'd pick up your men,
sloths, predators, crotched in an alley
to rhythms of bleating and sweat,
to the smell of cum.

My life has hung in our closet
with the clothes you left behind—
your chemise, your negligee.

I've crammed into your heels,
into your nylons,
rubbed them gently down
against my skirt;
padded cups for breasts,
glass diamonds
linked around my neck.

Sometimes I'd walk downtown
late at night in your coat,
the mock fur wrap
with the classy pin,
past Joe Ling's Bar,
past the sign
of the pawn broker's balls.

Finally, I lost my shame.
I chose your fanciest dress,
primped my wig, the binding one

I'd picked from the junk,
shaved my stubble, painted my lips,
powdered my wrinkles, and dared.

I walked down the steps into the morning,
greeted neighbors and nannies.
No one noticed. No one asked.

That evening I walked
through your alley
stacked with cats and vermin
and the stench of dreck.
Sewers belched their putrid gas.

I whimpered and swooned
just like you. I marked my time.

But no one called your name.
No one came to kiss my lips,
to touch my parts,
to give me pain, to watch me
squirrel and weep with joy.

No one came to hold my hand,
to take me home,
to whisper the words I'd learned
to hide my loneliness.
No one saw me.

If you were to understand what I mean,
you would have to acknowledge my fears.
Fallacies lie in all the corners of my room.
Foibles in my playpen.

You would have to watch my butterfly strokes,
my flights through the meadow, *Un paysage*—
a wonderful French word that wanders,
sweeping across the hem of my skirt,
landing in my lap, turning green with the weeds,
bright yellow in the pods of sunflowers
where I want to be born.

Were you to say, *You must,* you would be wrong.
You would *must* me climb that cliff
with no ballast, no way of saying, *Enough!*
I'm sweaty and tired and I want to go home.
You would have sent me, in your own gracious way,
to a precipice, alone.

And when you arrived boldly to the rescue,
how would you greet me? As a brother? A father?
A benefactor who thrives on giving and giving?
Should I feel helpless or only stunned?

amongst my failures, endless miles of faults,
that rise, fall back, pound,
drowning me in hysteria.
My fear is that of exposure,
of being unmasked by critics
who bore through my mind,
who, unbeknownst to me,
decipher my secret flaws.

I resist my fright with diversions,
fantasies
against my countless burdens
that cry for relief,

that wake me in the middle of a dream,
that feed me guilt and remorse,
that add to the reasons for having
to cling to your pity.

The Fifth Horse of the Apocalypse

He sees with no eyes
but holes, shrunken,
strung to a fusible mind,
a skull of caverns and portals,
twisted jaw, mane of wire strands,

with a spine, a saddle,
arched where a horseman used to be,
a belly of steel wool shrubs,
spindly limbs of spindly scrap,
tail corroded, stiff,
legs too weak to pull a dray
too diseased to care.

Left Behind

Burning
in the afternoon squall,
waves of gray geese
filled the distance,
seared by the sun,
driven down
against the wills
of their disfigured wings.

Their severed parts of speech
skewed the simplest verses
in the world,
straining to pronounce them
as if they were sweet.

If these verses were sweet,
I'd tell you
that their thrumming pain
burns less the more they bend.

But Time spirals inward.
Textures lose their waves,
collapse to shreds, to discord.

If they were pleasant,
I would laugh and say to you,

These flights are pleasant.
These geese are kind.

Their waves are fine.
Their verses, charming,

as I've been left behind
to float alone
where my planet used to be.

Forgiveness

I know three ways to speak of forgiveness—
    in enormous blasts of trumpets and flares,
    in faint glissandos,
    inside-out until my entire body drenches in trust.

I see only three ways to think of forgiveness—
    in shades of green and mauve,
    in fertile soil, relentless waves of alluvial silt,
    in the need for fidelity,
    for fealty, for comfort and love.

You speak of three, not two or four,
but three unwavering pleas by those who suffer—
    for solace in their grief,
    for relief from the torment of helplessness,
    for remorse by those who've fêted on dying,
    who've disfigured the living,
    who must work in perpetuo
       for the forgiveness of Time.

In a Sky of Horses

Wild horses dragged a woman
across a sky   too close
to the rim to the brink   to the corner
of the sun   of the planet Earth

                              millions of stallions
raced through countless meadows   ploughed through boundless gorges
trampling songbirds   spewing rage

Mercilessly raped   she clung to their backs
she clenched their manes   Dangling
she held fast   reaching
pleading   for the charity of heaven
                  crushed by the apathy of sleep.

Astronomic Correlates

I'm sure that suns devour their light,
involute at night and sleep, alone,
in their nudity, between sheets of rain.

If there exists a sun that rises and falls
by permission of the soul,
there can be no *infinite* beyond,
only fringes that remind us
of the breadth of our limitations.

Hurtling through time,
a sun will reach the limits of existence
then spring back, while the sky, itself,
appears content to live in peace
within the confines of its elegance.

Time compresses, racing towards me,
expanding as it flies away.
An instant may be reached,
a point through which it passes
that marks my dwindling to nothingness.

In the Hourglass on My Desk,

sand from the upper chamber
spills in a stream to the lower one.
Turned, sand having filled the bottom
becomes sand in the top
that spills once again to the bottom.

In this way, time flows both up and down,
forward and back,
buffeting the qualms in my future.

Parallax

If no sun exists
outside the space of time,
there can be no *infinite* beyond,
only the span of a life and its death.

So I ask you,
do suns devour their skins?
Is sleep nude?
Between linen sheets of drizzle?
Do they hide from their own elegance?

Since our moon streams light
from the sun obliquely
beyond the face of our planet,
how can it be truly be called full at all?

Of course. Light bends, distorting itself
to satisfy the shape of the universe.

But at the end of day,
why does the moon not glow scarlet,
iridescent, like the sun
and the thin cirrus strands
that blanket the skyline,
crossed here and there
by jet streams flying
from the ends of the Earth?

When will the sun burn out
and the moon grow dark forever?

Archipelago

The island night grew dark
with cutty boats,
sludge in their nets,
dried blood on their gaffs.

She climbed the slope
to the crater, pinnacle, crust,
seething with rape
through the hash of her life,
tearing her mind to shreds.

She climbed to the brink,
to the mouth
of smolder and fumes,
where the value of life
limps away into flame.

She patted her womb and laughed,
laughing loudly, sardonically,
again and again.
Her echoes spread across the sky
until there was no more rage to spill
and no more sky to soak up vengeance.

Her fears blistered. Her throat was parched,
her mind grew lame.

She raveled. She raved. But no one heard.
No one grasped her grief,
or the love she might have longed to kindle,
or the force of her leap into conviction.

We've Reached the Midriff of Our Marriage

when suffering occurs in small spurts,
when marriages float away unseen,
beyond one's ability to retrieve them.

What remains of affection
falls like the dead weight
of a virgin-like smile
that masks so well
with the gusto of the crowd.

We've spoken like courteous hangmen
at a time when a life is cheaply lost
each day at the bottom
of some friendly cup of tea.

We've counted conciliatory stones,
skimmed them across the appearance
of paper-edged innocence.

We've surgically cut into all species
of pride and kindness,
herding them, like bands of thugs
into dungeons to simmer, ferment.
Perched on our haunches,
we've smothered our frailties,
disguised our defeats
from each others' reproach.

Evenings glut us with stifled urges
preserved in thinly scripted myths,
that define the terms of our failure,
our callous retreat from the ones
we've grown to love.

Still, I need to tell you things
you may not want to hear.

Bonaparte Courts Josephine

at the Banquet of Waterloo.
Three wise men enter a cat-house
met by a sheepish grin
on the face of Madama,
a manikin embracing her pimp
with chapel vows.
Angels flit around each other,
up and upside down, waiting their turns
for ecstasy. An officionato enters.
An organ pumps a dirge.
The cherubs behave.
Josephine laid.
The marriage is made,
Bonaparte returns to his grave.

Temperence

Squeeze juice of ½ orange,
2 oz. dry gin, 1 oz. vermouth
1 oz. sweet vermouth
shake well with cracked ice,
pour into fish bowls, serve
with gardenias, hooks and sinkers.
Rivers flow out the door
into the sanctimonious night.
Croakers fall prey to one's fancy.

Bumps

Phrenology is the roadmap of life.
Heads bump into kisses that fly
from nose to ear. Numbered bumps
think serial kisses that fly together
into different parts of the body.
Bigger bumps are bunnies.
Small ones grow till they fuck,
then whimper and cry,
when all such antics
make them go mad.

The Coach *

I tell you, at the end of time
on the bell tower clock,
with each rumble, each hoof beat
that crosses our town,
spurred on by a teamster's ominous shouts
that whip his steeds to whinnies
that shatter the night,

streetlamps fail. An elder shrieks.
An infant gasps in his bed,
all with the glare of a moon
dressed in truculent green,
pasted on sheets of stars
that strike each roof in our village.

Cobblestones ring from the shearing force
of his iron-rim wheels, faster, faster,
spurred on by the cry of the madman
whipping his steeds, shattering the night,

spreading its fury with sweltering shock
from the anger of an Earth
that rolls to heaven
in the dust of a fungus cloud,
that will lose its place in the universe.

> * *inspired by prospects*
> *of a future nuclear disaster*

At the End of the World

A river separates two armies grown murky with mud.
Peace reigns by default between two wars.
In the season of drought, two banners vie for rain.
They hammer each other, succumb by Cause, die from Danger.

In the year of the Tempest, a heretic sea floods the land,
dragging its entrails through the sweet soup of glory.

Two hostile warriors battle for the love of Yahwey.
They speak His name. They slice Him into tasty morsels,
eat Him raw then sink in the loam together.
Bread and wine cover the Earth.
A crescent moon surrounds the sky.
All take leave of the universe.

It is Time to Understand

Mornings follow us
up the smoke soaked road
to the mill, to its belching stacks.

Porches fill themselves
with underwear and worn out shoes.
Soup bowls pour each night
for those whose aging
bring them loaves of grief.

It is time I tried to understand,
to crouch in a corner of my room,
to rid myself of frames of mind,
complexions, of cavils,
quibbles, grumblings,
mirror likenesses of my petty face
that hang around my stinted neck
like scarves that bind me
to the freezing summer heat.

My Fountain

At the foot of my city
at the foot of the day,
lies a fountain.
Do you know what I mean?

Narrow streets surround themselves
with rivers that run off into gardens.
Beneath the sky,
all shades of vibrant fugues and cantos.
Do you have any idea what I'm saying?

In rows of pyramids and pinnacles,
from bookshelves to echoed halls,
there lie repeating themes,
currents and contrasts
that mix sweat with endeavor
into themes of intention.

These seemingly disparate thoughts
wisp around my ears,
evanescent and often unnoticed,
caught in the spray from the fountain
that drenches my waking hours.

How can I tell you in a simpler way
what is on my mind?

Inexorable

You flee your shriveling
bladder and bowels,
your legs, lifted one by one
by your arms which, in time,
will not lift at all,
will not feed you,
will lose their strength
to greet me when I visit.

Your pleas beg a special
place in heaven—
pitching back and forth
in your slurries of speech.

You lose your touch.
Pain burrows through your bones.
Your pasted laugh belies
the fragmentation of your mind.

Your vision sweeps to the right,
grudgingly back to the left,
wandering through dark caverns
under miles of blinding snow.

You fall to strokes of a rocker
with its dubious comfort
that drags you to despair.

This ballerina has lost her shoes,
her skill to transpire.
She can no longer flee,
no longer squander herself
in the poverty of sleepless nights.
Too few nights.
Too severely few to come.

There can be nothing happy
in your torched grassland.
Flames inexorably
sweep your mind.
Hope fights fear.

Instead, in the biggest
stead of your life,
you must turn your passion
to delight. In fine curls,
and robes and veils,
you must laugh with splendor:
la pashadom, maharani,
malikzadi.
New stars will eclipse your mask,
forever fresh and vivid
in this opalescent world.

The Art of Affliction *

Once again,
you cover yourself
with a mournful face,
with a Doric column
for a spine, shown
through the gaping cleft
between your breasts.

You shed tears,
place pain in the palms
of your hands to mold
the shape of your suffering.

Rain pounds the red tile roof.
Drops coalesce as they trail
down your forehead,
your forest, your window panes,
distorting the world's loneliness.

Lead pipes bend your body.
Thorny leafless vines
poison your legs.
Wild dogs blacken
the tips of your toes.
They fall off
into a wicker basket
in the middle of the night.

An artist paints murals
to bury afflictions, sewn to secrets

under layers of oil-cheese gloss
on canvases stretched
to their limits in times of want.

And you are disfigured.
Your art becomes torture.
You cry in scraps of passion,
from fatigue.

An invalid wears a crown
to shield her from judgment
while she searches for a word
that means Hope, one that blooms
from a lemon tree with roots
that warm the frozen ground.

Lava surges from your slurry of moods.
A shadow touches your eyes
and places you in a helpless body
that feels mundane delusions,
and whimpers and whines.

You walk through a grieving field,
through a bed of convictions
with a voice of solid stone
and the eye of your lover
engraved on your forehead
to mark your despair,
to remind you of the man
you'd placed in a paper bag
and tossed away.

   from the art of Frida Kahlo

From My Life

I've dashed through alleys, windblown streets,
everywhere diluting, vaporizing space and time
(orbital ridges, ocular fossae, vision itself),
escaping the turbines that drive me
to pimp the bombast of night.

Trees in a gale
splinter their boughs to shreds
with bleeding wounds that cover
our plazas and parks. From this wreckage,
distorted men emerge who've reduced
their lives to dollops.

Subways stifle my howls.
Shrieking trains erupt into missiles.
I feel always fear
that I'll fall between their hungry tracks
with my bitterness.

Having run the distance alone,
having shed my stench behind me,
I'll sink into a wicker chair
in a beggar's flophouse on a wharf
by a poisoned river
and sing an old song while I die of rain.

Tough Tale

He hid inside
a thick shell of steel
of a man. Tough sinews
masked the ponderous
force in the shafts
of his bones.
Tough meat
on his bones.

And he worried
with his strand of beads,
chinking one
against the other
with his rusty hand
in the pocket
of his coat,

as he wandered,
wantonly trundled
through one to another day
and galloping night.

And he burrowed
deep down
to the velum
of his meaning,
to the shafts of his steel
of a shell, with the force
of his ponderous bones.

And he tried. But he failed.
With his hands in his rusty pocket
and his chinking strand of beads,
he failed.

Actress

Prions strut around the stage,
zyming torn pants drenched in sick perfume,
badgering and dickering and otherwise
bathing in the tethers of clandestine infidelity.

They stand firm on the photo of a vagrant.
He yelps only once. Not twice, only once:
          Marilyn, oh Marilyn,
            I'm cloned to protect you
            from the harm
            of your own dirty self.

Out the Door *

Rorschach's all, pouring heads of state from cans of soup
made twice as tasty on the bones of their shadows,
bathing in noodles with kinky bow ties.

Uncle Sam and Lady Godiva melt with a parting song.
God and His commandments leave me incredulous.

The scarlet sportster burns the macadam
dead heat, into a patch of berries.
Wrecked sedans pack up top in a ditch,
eating words with garlic, spilling great goodbyes
into heaps of cans of gumbo,

while into the slinky red pimpmobile we go,
with a cloud of dust and a hearty,

Ho-Hum Silver, away.

 * inspired by drawings and watercolors
of the erstwhile shoe designer, Andy Warhol

Dali Remains an Enigma

I watch a boy
on a canvas shore
lift a thin skin of surf.
Underneath, in its shadow,
sleeps his dog.

His dog drinks its shadow.
The boy, unperturbed,
becomes a girl
that skips her rope across the beach
for what is left of the light of day.

The face of a clock drapes itself
over the branch of a decimate tree,
ticking, counting minutes,
simply waiting for the painting
to come to an end.

I watch from a cliff beyond
until a voice rings out
and we all slink back to our rituals.

In the Queen of My Life

I'm a woman of wonder
in the queen of my life,
sprouted from the moon
on a street, a pavilion
turned bright
with dancing flares—

as if a handsome man
wrote his name
on my skirt,
singing his rhythms
to my womb—
as if my body leapt
to the dunes of his calling!

How many wonders
swim in the syrup
that teems from his crest,
from his fluttering specks
of grain!

I am the Birth of Sundays.
Exotic. Ecstatic.
I've climbed the sky
and waved my scepter
at the ice that masks
my Mother Moon.

I'll touch her knowing face.
She'll bend her light

to the crescent shape of my hand.
She'll melt a bit and smile,
then drop behind the skyline,
triumphantly to sleep.

Hieronymus Bosch

If tears were not symbols of want,
challenges not faults, defeats;
if rage was not a casualty of passion
and sequels, not replays in waiting—
But they are.

Each night, I reach to Hieronymus Bosch
and his murals filled with creatures
warped in puddles of slag.

I see myself amongst them,
never quite human, never not,
struggling to where two henchmen
might kill each other, a third,
immortalize their slaughter, and a fourth,
run naked through the streets,
shouting dung to senseless revilers.

Bosch has spread this ghostly truth.
And I? Conscripted into his band
of quasi hominids,
small and lonely and lost.

I've worked to mend the rents
in my veins, distortions stitched
in a house where a child might once
have been meant to bloom,
fresh and thirsty, loved and kempt.

But beauty hides its treasures
out of reach of the wanting,
who have never seen
the life of a child's smiling face
in the cage of a teeming zoo.

Cherry Tree

A cherry tree rose in a corner
of the meadow, her face chafed dry
by the wind. Her mane flowed jade,
like sails on a sloop
bounding giant crests in a sea of thistle and gold.

I'd have had her blossom in silk pirouettes,
swash her leaves on the knoll, dip them deep
in red flags of sunset.

But her roots held firm in sovereign soil,
nurturing her simply spoken tones.

I'll harvest those tones and string them, one by one,
like beads around my neck, beneath my scarf in winter.
I'll return in the spring, through the overgrowth
to find her agèd beauty.

I'll ask for her once more. If *no*, I'll leave in peace.

Kharma

Our footsteps printed our names
on drifts of virgin snow.
They led us through
forty-nine thirsty days
to arrive at a new time
in which to live.
I remember only the tilt
of a tree against the lilt

of a smile, laughter
against the loss of a child
against a frozen berm
that yielded to nothing
but the warmth
of our wedding bed
as we play tonight,
undaunted
by this pathos.

Front stage,

at a cultured cabaret in a drizzly city,
dancers, silver strutting steps
in netted hose, heels flung high,
miniskirts, slim sheik necks
with pretty faces closely shaven,
painted eyes, and lips,
perfect smiles,
halters bounding from their chests
with each exotic thrust,
wait to find their loving ones.

Soliloquy

To walk amongst
the spiders
who make music,

plucking strands
of their webs

like petals that point
from all the flowers

on which we so
unceremoniously depend,

like constellations
in a sky pocked with geese

in a flock of migrating winds
that scour the clouds for rain,

like a gentle woman who arrives
to free us from our burdens
and take us home to bed.

Nights of Cabiria *

You live in the mind of the night,
in an instant smile
made of finely ground trifles.
From darkness, you sway
to the very next street lamp
and into the arms of a john, into bed,
to search him with your touch,
till morning when you fall
again into facelessness.

Your "redeemer" caresses
the used part of your hand
in which you keep your kinks,
the grasp you use to wretch
at the parting of each new
jinny.

Tonight, your fur will float you
through the brawling cabaret.
Your piercing eyes will rule the evening.
Your effacing shrugs will wave flags
to the ghetto girls—
who would claw you to death
to take your place.

> * inspired by the film
> with Giuletta Masina,
> by Federico Fellini

Plague

His hat awry,
He walks across the bridge
beside the tracks
from one to another city.

It's not too hard to discern
purpuric people, desparate corpses
stacked together,
pulled through the rain
on donkey carts that cry
for more, in an orgy
that can best be described
as odious memories
of bitter red wine.

But red turns white in winter,
then black to soot.
Cities fall to famine.
People die. Do you hear?
People actually die
against their will.

His hat awry,
He might eat lunch
then cross the bridge
beside the tracks, look back
and wave goodbye.

Maria Sabina

When Maria Sabina died,
someone twisted the neck
of a rooster and laid it
by her side. On the fourth
day, not the third or the fifth,
its spirit rose up and crowed,
calling her soul to depart,
to start its journey
to the Dead Land
feeding on squash seeds,
greens and fruit along the way.

Someone lit a candle at her feet.
And on the fifth, not the fourth day
or the sixth, her soul rose
and folded a palm cross
through cow fields and cold streams.
She was neither thirsty nor hungry.
in her right hand
as it lay on her breast.

She followed the rooster,
dressed not in feathers
on the wings of a songbird,
but naked, without shoes,

On that day, in a single moment
of the moon, she felt fresh.

after *The Mythology of Mexico and Central America.*
John Bierhorst. New York, William Morrow.

Central Park

A swarm of office workers lunch on benches
in the park. Shrill horns from motor cars
compete with music from an instrumental group
of three, as they pass hats for alms.
An elderly woman sifts garbage,
sampling from trash cans,
from one to the next,
then back to her shelter
under the bridge in the zoo.

Millions of us
pack a park bench.
A hunchback hag
scavenges trash,
waste bin popcorn,
apple cores, and sopping butts.

A small boy smiles,
who, having almost
made the smiling-bond,
bounds away
as we pelt him
with glares we carry
in our pockets
for such pelting purpose.
We swarm from the park,
we docket drones.

Our park-bench lunch
sucks with chicken-drip-
finger-licken-chyle,
to the strains
of a sax-a-billy troupe
that pass a hat, their chat
to screech
above the dinning cars.

These men of music,
puckered lips,
split tunes
through brassy cones
tink their timbres,
sinking back
to their stricken homes.

While down the path,
she The-She
suckles worn out fruit,
wipes gravy
dripping down her sleeves,
her burlap blouse,
her glue-stained skirt.

Lying on the knoll,
clouds falling all around,
sopped, and shingled,
her eyes gaze up
to an elderly sky.
Wilted flowers
die in bins with trash,
never minding her never-mind.

Lightning rips
with savage brash.
She murmurs, cries.
She lies in a shattered peace
that eats at her grey
unknowing hopes, too crazed
to want to die.

At last, she folds her legs
to rest with a fag and a smile,
then saunters back to her snuggery
under the bridge at the zoo,
sniffing all the while our munching joy.

At the stroke of noon,
we'll spill again to the park
to our musical bench.
Our local horns will simmer,
our poor-shrift maid
will sift our trash,
slurp our salads,
with her vacant vacancy.

In waves, we'll end our lunches,
rush to the subways, down, then up
and into our cages,
hurried chimeras, restless limericks
locked in our post-bellum beds
until our days doom.

Dense Bushes

Have you ever flown from a parapet
with lead wings, raised a banner
that bled its way to half its mast
where it lived in effigy
for the rest of its life?

Have you raised your faith
from a vacant pulpit
to the very pinion of a spire,
to hear the toll of waning death
as He would want it to be?

In my sleep, I slice hot peppers.
My fingers tingle. I touch my eyes.
I see white pain. It travels lightning speed
through my orbits,
along my optic tracts that swerve
around the lining of my skull
to implode the back of my brain,
sending me forward in fugues
and figurines, to come to rest
in a massive sheet of tears.

I both soar and tunnel through the inferno,
in the throes of a thunderhead,
riding the exhilaration of fright,
mourning the loss of some incarnate totem,
while submitting to its hunger
that devours me with each emotion,

with each stroke of a pendulum
religiously sweeping its razor-edged arc,
through each cycle,
each surge of each throb from each limb
of each chamber in my heart.

Trite

I watched the moon
rise above the whitecaps
that lapped at the sediment
on the sand and its krill
and its crabs that scurried
like silver dollars from under
my feet along the beach
and into their burrows
and the deep orange light
from over the dunes
that illuminated nothing
only dripped condolences
softly on the surf.

Little Girl Blue

I see a little blue girl hold her dove to
        her breast. I watch
                her search for tender words. But then,
                we were once all children
belonging to a time when space was an
        obedient circle, when love was
                made of flakes descending on a sleepy
                yawn within a snow that
                        melted into springs that
                                triumphed, after all.

The Danube

Above all, I must tell you
about the state of my world.

The Danube is woven
into muddy brown fabric
with red suede roofs
that dot its banks,

with groves of ocher leaves
that stand on the backs of conifers,
puffs of squat yellow bushes
against poplars that shoot up,
straight, tall and thin
into the cold November,
saplings that bend
their roots into pools of sludge.

The waiter on our riverboat
says he understands
my request for tea.
The whiskey here is clearly
of the worst kind.
Diluted as well.
Yes, he is quite correct.

Our guide now firmly shouts,
We are crossing into Germany.
Everyone.

See the gingerbread homes.
She is also quite correct.

My wife faces the spray.
She returns with the crystalline smile
on the face of our guide's assurance.

We reach Cologne
with its cramped cobbled streets
and tinkling gift stalls.
Regalia casts itself in bronze.
A renaissance General steps down from his plinth,
with his medals, on his haunches and heels,
to gift us a generous slice of palaver,
a salute to tourists
who feed their ambitions each day
on his extraordinary sense
of the thrill. Again and again.
He is always right.

The Danube is forever woven
with red suede roofs.

The Lover

I've poured myself into a bottle
in that corner of the room,
that bulges with the syrup of rhetoric,
exploding into an ecstasy of anger.

I've shaped dominions that drip
from the globe, stalked constellations,
drowning them in fountains of gin.
Each time I murder your mirror,
shatter parts that show you nude,
I preserve some slivers and murder again.

I rob you of your kindness.
I maim your thoughts and feelings.
I wade through your trivia,
eat your slab of würst, your rind.
I sweep you into bed
and douse the lights in your honor.
and you take me for a friend
as if I were friendly,
as if you owed me
a portion of yourself.

In Barcelona

I sailed for Barcelona
by the sea, ancient sea,
taking rooms to sleep there.
Surly, surly, surly,
my jodhpurs perched
where the faithful stay,
plucking little fish-like fillets,
popping in and out to pray.

I met a gracious lady
to my infinite delight.
Abandoning the day,
we wallowed in the darkness
of a chocolate-covered night.
She touched my lips with orange rinds.
Our bodies climbed
to where our wishes dwelled,
to where our swishes
swelled in pools of simple sin,
our spirits bent to hear the sweetness
of a renaissance that sang
its passionate cadenzas,
voluptuous chagrin.

Like scything through the tundra?
Like waltzing cross the crescent veldt?
Like waddling up from penguin dunes,

"Fairies" in the Tasman Sea,
their silly, silly, silly,
molting with their midget spouses,
shedding little skirts and blouses,
bouncing back from wall to wall,
to waltzing in their swaddling beds,
to bathing in their watersheds.

She roused me,
popping in and out with play,
plumping little fish-like frizzles.
My jodhpurs crest where the faithless lay,
virally, virally, virally,
taking rooms, rigadoons,
to sleep by the sea,
then tacitly sailing away.
The Banker

An old man shuffles
his cart of rags
past every
shop front doorway
on the street.

With the rising
of a sallow moon,
a torn pair of undies
shines before his eyes.
Half blind with sheer delight,
he packs it into his bag
for the one he loves
so much.

Rooster

A rooster crows.
He cocks his jelly-red comb
throwing forward his neck,
and fluffs the feathers
on his breast. He cries
to the wind that sops up
the terror in his voice.

One forbids fateful thoughts
to shatter our cheerful
hides and seeks, our ruse
that Death is not a death at all,
but a long deep sleep
from which one arises
neither wishful nor sad,
neither grateful
for having come alive,
nor humble for the debts
owed to others,
only poly-pristine,
pure, and heaven blessed.

At dawn the rooster will crow.
He will dig at your tomb,
scratching dirt
with his scaly pronged claws,
weeping into the trough
he has plowed, to find you,
to tell you that he loves you still.

Origins

Have you ever lived in a three cornered hat
with a lamp that hung from the heavens,
a tricorn, shedding light of all dimensions,
reflected in your eyes?

I met myself for the first time in a portrait
in a sick hall of fame, in a circus
of hollow confessions marked to trap me
by gods more clever than mine,

with prayers from a church
dangling three corners of the sky away,
on an evening with the fragrance of spring.

I live in the needle of a prism
reflected in my eyes.

Raise the Red Lantern*

An aged woman kept the palace.
A single soul, silent,
the only living thing in sight.

We passed by portraits
        in The Courtyard of Maidens,
                one chamber garnished

each night with a red paper lantern
        for the coming of the lord.

The chosen mistress donned her silk lace gown,
        prepared her bed
                in diaphanous pleats to herald his visit.

She bore his covetous grasp,
        the impassioned stealth of his hands.
                Her lips drew wide by his thrusts,

with no shriek, only gracious hate
        for the regal chance to bear him a son.

We came to the Chamber of Savage Sleep,
        an ancient tomb, hollow and dark,
                that swallowed spent mothers

and the lives of their daughters,
        waste from the master of the house,
                for the pleasure of its Demon God.

My dear one is dead,
   transformed into gold in my pocket.
   And I bleed from my heart
     into the palms of my hands.

*Inspired by the film Raise the Red Lantern,
directed by Zhang Yinou, 1991.

Naked Tree

A slender tree stands
by a blue Krishna.
Two boughs.
Each
entwines a turbaned young man.
Each
beckons the maidens
of the village to approach.
Each
maiden skims the ridges
of flowers that float
across the garden, with the hem
of her robe.
Each
perfect star rises gold
against the azure light
that illuminates the village.

The Sax

Your saxophone stings
with its buggary,
with its slippery
mellow wander,
rose red cheeks
tensed wry, crying
to be heard.

Saxabillies moan,
wailing sand-grit
burr weed,
riding their souls
from the underground
to the tenth ceiling
of the sky with cries
above our claques
of sweat and soot,
streamers, trolleys,
chancres, morgues.

Wetted reeds bop
in a band,
strewn on a strand,
stretched up and down
the rubber riverside.

You cannot stop your sax.
Impossible. In crowds
on cobbled streets

rung with bungling,
with dirges dipped in biers,
in hot air vessels flaming
at the whoop of the wind,
you cannot stop its anguish.
You cannot stop its schmerz.

Parting

When your body parted
    flown like a dandelion

in the clothes of a cherry
    peppercorns
    tingled my fingers

Each word of yours
    whetted my mind
    quenched my thirst

seeded clouds that cleared the air
    of fluff and debris

swashed me
    like a new born pebble

saving our years from their ages
    as my anger learned
    to miss your touch

Beggary

I

Begging requires the fine touch of a master
invented by his tools;
a crumpled hat before him on a sidewalk,
a limp, contempt for a fortune
he had never had the mind to acquire,
potato mash at the Salvation Army
post or station or kitchen
for homeless endeavors.

A beggar must be held immune
from disgust;
an unwilling member
of a proud gang of thieves,
he has not yet learned to rob.

With the elegance of homelessness,
he must crow like a cock in a barnyard,
asking, pleading,
beseeching each passerby to touch him
with a coin or a dollar bill.

No matter. He was raised in a pot of dung soup
where he awoke to find he'd drowned
and could not scream.

And when he dies,
he'll not have to pay for lodging in hell,

only fawn his way into heaven,
pawning himself
for a meal and a glass of grog,
and a god without a name.

He will live forever on the stones of graves
where he was born, always pleading,
crumpled hat, for a place in our lives.

II

I tumble out of bed with the birth of dawn,
doffing to gentlemen, tripping at the sight
of fanciful ladies.

I work the crowds in my vagrant suit
and fawning smile.

Ambition? To afford a Sunday afternoon.
My mortal fear? To wake in the morning
without the cane and cup
that make me delicately blind--—
to rise to the ranks of those
who curse all beggars,
like to amputate their arms and feet,
destroy their magic touch.

Beethoven

It's fulfilling to feel the martyr
even if you can't remember
the cause he espoused.

Alone, as if to pray at some shrine,
I'd meet my heroes
in their narrow escapes from death,
and the pretty maiden, Claire,
the kid down the street
whom I saved from the fiery dragon
almost too vague to remember.

There were nights I sat on the piano bench,
under the tutelage of my father,
playing poorly, until, when, fatigued,
he'd smack his little cretin
and send him to bed. Somewhere
he must have been tender,
by the smoothness of his hand.

It's a powerful feeling
to own a space inside yourself,
sensing it belongs to someone great.

My name was Beethoven.
His father was mine.
He was heroic, triumphant.
I was triumphant.
I know, in my dotage,

that Claire remains five,
and I save her each day
for the rest of my life.

Blind Man

Past the lamp down the path
by the hedges to the steps,
each step that creeks,
splinters in the fragile
course of time—

How did you find your way?
Did you kick the pebbles,
sense the soil and the berries,
smell the manure,
hear the robins' sing?
Did you whiff the lilacs
and the hyacinths?

How did you manage the porch,
avoid the rocker, find the door latch?

You've returned to the same broken home
with the same drawling gables
and windows, drapes slit in lengths,
tied in knots to be stripped and discarded,

with the shadow of the chimney
in the late afternoon and the lilies
that float on the pond
in the gaslight by the smokehouse,
the chubs, the ripples that lap
the shoreline in the fading warmth
of a dwindling sun.

If I cut you some blossoms,
can you conquer your dark?
Might you grasp some devotion
in what I have to say?

Family History

My brother bore toxins
that seeped from his seemingly
dormant wounds,
that poured each day
through his presence,
crusting the face of his years,
driving his ego to its death.

I reached for the sounds
we'd shared
before we were taught
to strip to our fingers
and hands, our fascia,
muscles and bones,
to wash them horribly clean—
before, when we first cried for love.

To Design a Face,

you must saw through a bough on the north side
of a great alder, on the wet side of a winter's day.
  Watch the tree twist and bend toward its phantom limb,
    its brown bark peel back to an ivory sheen
      dripping sweet sap from its eyes.
        Listen closely, your ear against its cheek.
        Hear its cry. Collect its fallen leaves.
          Place them in your purse for tomorrow,
            with regret.
By God.
You must regret what you've done!

Bear in mind your child was born on a wintry street.
The wind caught you both in a portrait of

  Mother Caressing her Infant in Snow.

Watch for his instants of his self-consciousness,
  his delicate reach,
    his search for his own place in life,
  his senses and solos
      and the terrible things
        he will be moved to do
          through his years
            to prove his worth.

To design a face, you must cross the field
    to the wreath on the grave where your lover fell.
        Lie beside him with the prospect of being together forever.
       Find a strip of sod to cover you.
            Think of what he must have surely been through.
          Wake him gently and ask.

You must stroke across a canvas with a swath

    of decimate red, brushed over
       by a sudden ray of light the timbre
         of an orchestra with the force
                of youth's magic horn.

Watch the doves and crows and sparrows and cardinals
    who have always painted their cheeks before breakfast.
       See the clouds arrive on time. Fly into their froth.
       Prop a rainbow on a picket fence
        and ask me to repeat my funny dance
       where no one else can see.

Then command yourself to grow old and cloister.

The postman will hand you a letter
with a small paper stamp
from the widow in the house next door.

You'll read it. You'll hide it. She loves you.
You'll hurry through the streets

on a moonlit night to the sandbox
in the playground in the park.

You'll draw with a twig all the wrinkles in her face.
You'll drink each motif you learned
since the childhood of your birth.

You'll capture your shambles and triumphs,

prepare yourself for the advent of your birth—

an enormous event!

Vigil

You built a daunting ship
and ploughed your story of the sea.

You added courage to frailty,
larger, much mightier than hope.

Your ship split and splintered
by the force of a gale, smashed
to its gunwales on the slopes of Dover.

I placed a light in the window,
waiting for your story to return.

I sank into the rocker
from where you took your trips.
I found you on the page of Job.

Now, I speak to your shadow,
place two lights in the window.

Tomorrow, I'll walk to market
and buy the cliff
that gave you your story.

I'll place it gently in my purse
and walk home.
Each night, I'll play the wind
on which you dreamed yourself away.

My Father

Curious how we lose our charm
when we shed our feathers.
Then there are the mildewed secrets,
closet scriptures,
visions of clandestine rendezvous
with sweethearts, kinky women,
beefy men, impresarios, maestros.
So many encounters
spill over the brim of one's years,
with the drive to forgetfulness,
to survive at least
until tomorrow morning's tea.

Evening dragged the old man up to sleep.
We climbed the stairs
furrowed by tracks of shoes
that had smeared a trail to the top.

His room set off a stink
that dribbled down the walls,
down his sleeves
to the palms of his hands.

His words came garbled,
sprawled across his bed.

An "El" passed the window,
its rails raised on iron stilts
above the street. It shrieked

at the top of its lungs,
barbarous, brazen,
racing headlong around the corner
to the next station, filled with ghosts.

The old man paused.
His right hand trembled.
His left hand wiped away his sweat.

Elegy

For my father

Your fury has failed.
But your chest still heaves,
then stops, then hesitates,
drawn back, then heaves again.
And your strength still pounds
your heart with each sigh.

Your eyes tarnish
beneath the weight of your lids,
palms still streaked with coal.

Your dreams must be sifting
the handful of coins
that held us together
when famine
ate the bread from our plates,
when corn was only a pod
of rotten stalks and sheaths,
when night drew darker
than ever before,
lost to hopelessness.

The whistle sounds
for a change of shifts.
Stacks burn on.
Their afterglow
breaks into overcast.

The wind turns East.
Soot clears from the hills.
There, your friend awaits
with his smile and his stallion,
to carry you off
to his haven in Dead-land.
      Go in peace.

Elegy

For my mother

Your grace has died,
breaths meek and shallow,
fitful, slipping away.

Many times you were hurled
from misogynous cliffs,
gaffed by stigmas that lurked below.

You leached into canyons,
rivers rife with taunting jeers
from hollow throats,
their elegant howls of junk.

Your shoes no longer walk
beneath the hem of your skirt.
Your hair, no longer garlands.
Your heart still twists on its root,
dwindling with each drubbing stroke.
Death will sing forgotten words
when Hell is razed
in the house of heaven.

The String

Years grew taut
around the strains
in her face,
loving tones in her eyes,
voracious bowings
up, then down,
fragments of sotto voce,
gritting thrusts
from threads
of her existence.

Irrelevancies gone,
distortions lost,
there came the purity
of flags and flaunts,
through years of reaching
for the uttermost string
with a timbre
high above the range
of my power to grasp,
with a softness that spoke
to the havoc she'd seen.

Daybreak

In the broadest sense
this is a trustworthy place
in which to live.

> Courage never meant
> the absence of cowardice
> but one's burning need
> to engage.

I rise into a menagerie of pretenses
that drive my delusions forward.

> Your face may be vague
> but your contradictions
> uncover your urge to exist.

What is that supposed to mean?

> You smile.
> You greet me.

I think of a beautiful scripture,
but I cannot quite read the words.

Verses jumble; the poet gone.
Yet, there is a sense of belonging.

> I hear the drub of the foghorn
> of a scow that plows the river
> that laughs in the pummel
> of a violent storm.

Too Few Moments in the Gallery

Eyes are given to turning down.
Yours turn mauve with a light
that reflects the tears
that scroll down your face
in small moments
that hardly move at all..

I need those moments
to linger by the scar
on your cheek,
deep in your 1,2,3 layered story.
Pain appears
at the corners of your lips.
Enigmas shape your smile
on the pliant side
of your wilderness.

Then there's the rose that was not,
but should have been placed
in your hair,
so I could tell you by name.

Still, I would capture your nuances,
calling you to sleep in my garden
where roses are a treat
and dark eyes unheard of—
certainly when caring has died
and nothing on Earth is left to love.

To My Woman

No, we've not come to bed
to sleep,

> *shoulders firmly pressed*
> *against time on the clock*

Fireflies
will never cease
to speckle the night.

their fingers bristling,
kindling dangling us

You and I have strung
our wooden bows,
our feather-shafts,
launching them swiftly
with brass tipped
lightning speed.

We've axed our sorrows
like woodsmen in penance,
sweating through dense forests,
through blue-green sage,
saplings, and spider life.

We've summoned
ten heavens
of the mandarin duck,

floating on the sway
of our bodies,
painting our lips
with crystal calm,
wafting in and out
our tremulous thirst.

We've found
in those heavens
our Da Vinci limbs
winging the currents,
miming and feigning

through the freshening air,

playing together

to the end of each day,

each day prodding our play,

leading us to follow

each other to safety
             shoulders poised
             against voracious winds.

The Waltz

When does pain not grow dark?
When does dark not have its way?

Obtuse as it might seem,
does a piercing word, like lightning,
not shatter a rainbow,
splitting its hews
as it dies behind the skyline?

I cry. But you laugh yourself
into contortions,
an atrocious laughter
that echoes the guttural sounds
that rush from your lips.

When my body hurts
to the scalding point, it shrivels.

It sews wreathes
around my precious moments,
turning them to gold.

How many wreaths
before I sink beneath the loam?
How many hopes to smother me
in your words?

When I reach for a sound,
you shatter my story,

deny me my voice.
You waltz to the heat
of the limelight.
You bow with a lethal spear
in your hand.
I must cringe, burst with resentment,
 or find a way to hide my rage.

And Lastly Alexander,

does my pain
not show through my blouse?
Would I not have wished
to find a better way
to give myself to you?

Is there not a diva, growing old,
having sung enchantingly,
who, one day,
must swallow whole
her voluptuous voice,

or a dancer bent on waltzing
who must drag a grotesque shadow
of her steps across the floor?

Have I not reached to the lofty spire
for the warmth of a human touch,
to better mend a stricken bond?

Alexander,
I'm ready now. I'll remove my blouse.
You may fondle my breast. It won't infect you.
Neither will it send you on your way.
Nor bring you back.
Nor can I recognize its owner.
Nor can I pay homage any more to you,

having left me to struggle
against myself, alone.

Homeless

Come, little boy.
Show me the scar
on the right half of your face,
your open wound
that begs a spoon of succor
and a slice of caring bread.

Show me your rage, child, the anger
that stalks beneath your smile,
your empty arms, withered limbs
that bend to cover the rancid years
burnt into your body. Thwarted.
By every human measure,
robbed of the sacred salve
we need to live.

Show me the left half,
the blind eye that gazes
out beyond your reach,
the one that lost itself
in meshes of webs
of tangled threads of twine,
caught behind a window
that sees only spicules
the shape of sand.

Now show me your third half,
the one that drives your struggle
to conquer the syrup of submission;

that flies the trails that stream
across the heavens, sheer and strong
like tempered steel
that stands against the force
of the western wind, that sews
each scar to bring
your shattered life together,
that gives you the grit of compassion.

Goodbye

You'll point to a fine line
between the glint
of an angry moon
and a flood of passion,
between the pride in your psyche
that shines on the mantle
and the helpless pleas that fill
the gown you left
last night on the floor.

You'll tell me about the difference
between gazing from the porch
at our past, and the scarf
that drapes your shoulders
to keep you warm.
Then you'll tell me goodbye.

Goodbye is a frozen word
that will not melt
for a million years.
And when it does,
it won't lift a leaf to relieve me.

I'll nurse my anger chocked
with pods of contagion.

I'll take your hand
on a rusty winch raising buckets,

drawing water from a well
that has learned to spread disease.

I'll teach you the difference
between shackles, sorrow,
and the wish to live.
Then I'll listen to everything
you have to say.

Do you know

when you landscape,
your arms grow ferns,
your fingers fork with blossoms,
your voice roams the wildwood,
grows on oaken boughs,
that celebrate your new found diction?

I was stunted when I was born,
shriveled in my mother's womb,
actually died a whole death—
delivered, a stump of wilted ferns,
oaken fingers in wildwood

with the blood-red cord
still tight around my neck—
a timid weanling, searching
for a given name.

I Purchase Joy

I'm not pretty,
having suffered
boundless assaults
with padded clubs
disguised to look
like badges of glory,
filled with hidden omens,
excrement
dancing through the chambers
of my heart.

I've been taught to tell you
that resurrection cures wounds,
conformity, forbearance, pain.

Instead, I purchase joy
at the price of restraint.

I fawn. I slosh. I beg
some sham forgiveness,
reviling my pride each day,
smearing it with cultured pangs
of contrition.

Remember me,
not as I might appear tonight,
not by the price of my joy
or my portrait of guilt and fear,
the toll of my existence,

or the rage that hides
in my shallow smile
that hides my broken spine,

but by heart-shrieks
from a voice that bounds
yet says nothing.

You must tell this to my children,
Angel, William,
William, Angel.
They were younger than I
and I hardly knew them.

Rice Paper Wings

Have you never owned
a pair of rice paper wings?
I hide mine under my bed.
I write. I fill it with news
from all kinds of kids.
Fortune cookies tell me
I deserve good things.
When I get one,
I paste the message
to my wings to tell me
how well I can fly.

Do you know the difference
between a wing and a kite?
A kite has a tether and a tail.
It sneaks up from behind.
It wags. When the wind dies,
it brings you down.

Sometimes I have no pain
and don't need my wings.
Then, sometimes,
I don't feel strong enough
to bring them out
from under my bed.
That's when the tail
of the kite haunts me most.
It fills me with terror.

Lingering

I've learned that longing needs a glass of water
     and a thumbnail sketch
in an endless memory where maples,
     leaves still red, laden with snow, drip ice
on the road. By the west wall of the grove,
     crocuses
burst their casings and begin to sprout.

Still, I cannot find you in the dimming,
     behind the lace that combs your black hair,
that melds with the seizures in your eyes—
     at the very same moment that I see so clearly,
the red maples cry.

River Red

I've come to a place
that reinvents itself each night.
I scale the cliffs
that line the River Red below.

I wade through its caverns
amongst tiers of stalactites
that crush in my hand

to bits of chalk
that form beautiful words.

I feel married to all the centuries
into which I've been born,

delivered carefully on a flagstone
table of water, to find my way,

to follow the texture of the ground
on which I walk each night,
for the very first time.

Pashmina

Sorrowful words
dress themselves
in laurel to hide from grief.

Yellow-purplish flowers
show their pathos,
wrapped in wanting.

Beauty lay amongst
the trees, in the shack
where she built us a child,

Pashmina.
We gave her a knitted shawl
to sing her to sleep,
to guide her
in the art of wandering—

Pashmina.
I say our daughter's name
once more for the tears
that shepherd my woman
wherever she goes.

The Question

I've watched you fade,
slowly, gradually,
feeling your pallor
with the palm of my hand.

You know, some birds marry
sing the same song
fly rhythmically together

But your question? Vanished.
The answer? Gone.
It cannot sing or cry
or raise me when I stumble,
swollen, waxen, trickling,
stuttering, counting words
by their vowels
as if they held something
more for me to understand,

They collide with reflections
of their mates in the window

leaving me to grieve,
which I want so very much
to learn to do.

Through the window

at the snow capped
fountain in the park,
bundled people turn to ice
in their tracks trudging home.
Shadows stretch the streetlamps
down to the tracks of the passersby.

If you can imagine an orchard,
farm or mill, peach trees
in a field that needs scything,

if you can see a young woman
with wild, wild hair, flaring skirt
and loose blouse, loving herself,

tensing her body to take its great leap,
resting on a bank of milkweed,
turning to the gathering clouds,
swishing the scrub dancing home,

if cold breeds warm,
if colors are contrasts
and life innate and inevitable,
if you are the smile on your face
and the frown in the snow,
then climb beside her,
head on her pillow.
Reach for her beauty.
Bury yourself in the moment
she must leave.

I'm Glad

She slipped away to the ravine,
to the brink, muttering
in splintered phrases,
I've found my colors and I'm glad.

Vacancy lodged in the depths
of her glassy eyes.
Her voice raced down the chasm.

Whimpers carried her pleas
with the wind.
She cringed in the mouth of a flurry,
shuttering, stumbling back and forth,
wrapping herself in quavers.

...and I'm glad, she insisted,
without the slightest thought
of my presence, my coming
to snatch her and carry her home,
my holding her close
to fight her delusions,
rocking her back and forth
through the afternoon, into evening,
followed by night.

The Asylum

Matted floor, padded walls,
food from a tray
through a hole in a door
that rusts on its hinges.

Head in hands,
you rock slowly back and forth.
You burst with shreds of sounds.
You swing your limbs with indignation.

Sabers in your eyes,
rancor through the hole
in the rusted door,
pathos lain across your rage,

you ask me the cost of a human life.
You digest my feeble reply
in the sanity of your cell,
in your fervor and your strength.

Can't You See?

My wife died last night.
I saw my God,
God of Dawn,
where you're standing now.

Leaves of an alder
shrivel dry into rust.
Rust falls from the trees.

Birds peck at ripe cherries
they strip to stones.

Pain struck swiftly
in between the sheets.
Her lids closed.
Silence stalked, scraping away
at her consciousness
down to a deep set sleep,
on the last of our nights together.

Physician

Each day forewarns of the next.
My medicinal mouth winds rhetoric
like toffee that stretches taut
between my mind and my powers to heal.

By night, I dream of candles
spawning blue beads,
orange flags that waver and prickle,
that die of pain in the morning.

My tenets, they guide me
through the tyranny of doubt.
With vigor and hope,
they exhort me to search
for selflessness.

My spine,
my slacking shoulders,
splintered fingers turn to knobs,
thoughts into salvage,
fragmented,
caught in the pitch
of ruthless storms
floated out on riptides
of confusion—
They wake me, frightened.

Perhaps death comes swarming

like carpets of blackbirds

driven hard against the frost,
searching for food and warmth,
calling me to pack my books,
my bags, and join their flock.

Over the ridge,
I'll meet the Yijing prophets.
I'll bathe in rains that cleanse the air
with visions of peace and delight.

Meanwhile, you, young friends,
reaping each affirming instant,
bearing iridescent visions

sewn somewhere to the rucksacks

in your minds,

and you, old friend,
sauntering back and forth
in your soft white gown,
gazing through the tinted window
of ambivalence, waiting for me to enter,
to smile, to drop the first words—
This time, I can't.

The House I Live In

Helplessness thrives on deprivation.
Suffering spawns a meager way of life.
Struggle drives us to purpose?

I shrink to strings of whimpers,
plead to ease my pain.
I fall from life without glory,
without the fanfare of a bugler's tattoo.

Pulpits implode with prayers
by those who have not learned to kneel,
but stuff their pews, instead, with ambition.

I do not want to be king,
realizing that with power
comes also great danger and death.

Instead, I live in a modest house
in a tree in a forest.
I cut a stump in a clearing
on which to sit and ponder
the tall slender pines,
the warblers and the moles.

I place a stamp on a letter
I mail each day
that tells me how surely safe I am.
I marry my tears and tribulations,
while I struggle to be freed.

I swam for many years

through the eyes of my Father
in a world too strange
for me to understand—
with breasts too small and tears
that leaked through sieves,
drop by drop, to drown me
in my need to be beautiful.

Profundity spars with trivia.
My prayers were buried
in a single syllable of faith,
lost in useless credos, gravures,
profused with maxims
that prepared me for my guilt in Hell.

He followed me with His eyes
as if I'd been made to live solely
by the strength of benevolence.

This poem is by way of a useless cry
from the remnant of a mind
that is losing itself each day to depression,
nursing the temerity to die.

Myrtle Grows Forever

Most children grow brown bags
and orange wings,
itch behind their masks
and chirp on Halloween.

But myrtle grows forever.
And when I lent myself to you,
it was precisely from elegance
(brown bags, orange wings),
not from a dream
I'd bought to pander your need.

Elegance forgives, not for vanity,
but for the shear might of it.
And retribution?
For the sake of candor,
I have loved too much to sin,
to cheer as I weep,
to flee as I turn away.

My City at Night

I've grown up in brick and mortar stalks
that scratch at hanging cliffs of clouds,
that vie for sunlight on streets
that chew all things that cross them,
face all pain with equanimity.

Friendships forge by nuance,
eyes wide with the need to feel swarthy.
Taxis and cops and tin cups
beg through rains of parades.

The coin of the crowds?
endurance,
and statues in bronze, in marble,
invectives that fly with the sounds
of heavy steps on angry days.

I sit by a window over a ledge
on the eighty sixth story,
looking down through the smog
at strangers who might otherwise shun me
for my ugliness and the simple things
I have to say. They can't see me at night.

Swansong

Will you remember my gestures,
my body, my steps,
my silver sheen?

My love lies in the grace
I've been able to give you,
never knowing whether I'd live
by the velvet curtain
or reel on an empty stage.

And now, a slow studied step,
a cultured bow low from the waist
to those of you who've applauded,
who've found my dance appealing,
whose acclaim I cannot see
beyond the footlights, only hear
in the dark.

What makes a body think
it can always be greater than it is
when old age makes it smart
to its tips from pain?

Lights are not as blinding
as delusions they bring
to roles that one plays,
to one's faith in great music
that flirts with its tinge of display.

Still, you will never know how much
I thank you for your presence,
for your faith, and for the rose
I've pressed in my playbill
to remember you by.
You will never understand.

Subway

When a train speeds into the station,
two lights and a whistle
emerge from the tunnel,
whooshing lightning speed,
with a rush of stale air.
It looks at me angrily,
regards me with contempt.

The roar of the train grew closer
and louder, streaming past my face.

Screeching to a stop, it slapped open
its doors to engulf a crowd,
then quickly clamped them shut,
two guillotine blades
that would just as soon
leave half a person behind—
captives, we, in a missile in a tube,
like a string of torpedoes poised
to launch into the depths of the sea!

I squeezed amongst the crowd,
abutting the body parts
of a young stranger
in the next world away.
We swayed with the contours
of our bodies to the rhythm
of the wheels and their clacks.

He must have thought me
a rick of bones, unaware of the way
I curled my warmth around his eyes.

We arrived at my station.
The doors snapped open. Passengers out.
I bumbled up the steps to the street,
leaving behind my handsome new "friend"
whom I'll never see again.

I count the chuckholes,
pass the tangled brick buildings
to my flat, my wicker chair,
my lumpy bed, a lonely bed
that waits for my body
to sink in its folds.

Only once have I been loved
by a callused hand
that stroked back the hair
from my forehead
in the middle of the night.
Only once.

To the Zoo

The thought of death has cast me
into stories, into myths like,
Who's afraid of Virginia Wolfe.

Others deny their ages,
permitting them to live forever.
Still others suffer many years
longer than themselves
through the grieving
at their Yarhtzeits.

But I've moved through a fog
melting into my tumor with the grace
of a child who hides her pennies
in the darkest places, waiting for,
always having dreamed of the bus
that will stop by her bed, open its doors,
and take her, one day at a time, to the zoo.

Hyde Park

At noon on Sunday, a zealot rants
from a soapbox. His eyeballs bulge.
His heart bleats into a tin cup of pennies.

He reaches for his rage,
points to an abandoned church,
to a dissident defenseless old man
hung by his neck from the steeple
atop the burned out City Hall.

Lightning slashes holes in the clouds.
Roars break through his rhetoric.
His bellows announce a colossus,
the coming of the end of our world.

His zeal molds the crowd into a mob
of blisters lanced here and there
by his cunning, clumped together,
smeared with his slogans and lies.

Brazened and frightened,
people face each other's other
and begin to agree.

Rampant concurrence breeds bigots,
broken links of twisted chain,
skeins of leaded yarn, deranged loyalty.
Banners march with the verve

and brash of cattle,
blind to the scent of their slaughter.

Veneration turns to worship,
rapture to vows. Vigils shine.
Polemics drown us all
in dins of facelessness.

A child stands on the corner of a street
hawking news, Sunday News,
tragic news for sale! *Buy my news.*
Buy the hostile times
in which we buy our times.

We grab his hand and hurry him home.
We peel the fonts from under his nails,
the smile from his querulous face,
and send him promptly to bed without dinner.

Rejection

My lungs will rasp one day,
gasp to remind me of the droughts
that sank into evening
and the barbs on the lips
of my emptiness.

I see nothing beyond the moment.
I will die from an alien plague
in a puff of night.
Your face will kill me.
The expressions on your face
will drive me mad.

Nothing

A razor strop screamed
home across the incredulous
face and cheeks of buttocks
of a child,
crazed by the barbarous sounds
that raced through his room
in a vomit of destitution,
in a toilet that reeked
of the waste of human nothing
but his mother's anguished cries.

Each day he trickled down
the long narrow mirror
from his bedroom to his hell.

He found his father' gun
and thought to aim, to squeeze,
to slowly trip the trigger,
then vanish into darkness
leaving no trace more to harm.

But, you see, I no longer lived
when I was born.
Nothing had ever happened;
enormous tanks of nothing I could kill.

In the Lobby of the Old Hotel

I look up from my couch
in the railway station
to an arched rotunda. Blue medallions
encircle its dome. Light drips
in pellets that pierce the frosted roof.
Gaslights burn by the bar.

Kate Smith, I hear your voice
surrounding this open space,
echoing from a disc
in that wooden booth
with its old style telephone
hung off its hook.

All kinds of waxen flowers
grace the fountain in the center of the lobby;
zinnias, lilies, berries and twigs
in a cut glass vase with inlaid words,
in hardly intelligible French,
"I have loved you so much
in flaming beige."

Over there, see the curio china,
porcelain blue, pink bunnies,
and a rusted kiddy cycle
with a rusted seat and a rusted kid.

Beads string like planets
around the neck of an elegant woman

in her oval portrait on the wall.
Obsessively, she ruffles
her daughter's curls,
who mindlessly stretches across
her lap, with an opulent smile
of white death on her pretty face.

Adolescence

I

Streetlights fail.
You're blotted out.
Your shadow disperses
into powder particles of night.
I hate you. When you're gone,
I hate you even more.

I'm writing this poem
because I need a cause.

I want to be oppressed,
shunned, degraded, defaced,
left behind. I must cry
and look wanting
with plastic tears
across my face.

The doorbell often rings
at eight o'clock.
The door will swing open
on its hinges.

You'll enter. I'll watch you
cross the living room,
set you on my mantle,
crave to shout your name.
But you won't want to hear
a thing I say.

II

What is the sense
of meaning
when I have always to change,
when islands erupt
in random seas
and riptides spread
through random currents;
when silence scatters my vision,
bursting with mixtures of colors
caught in tectonic shifts,
a kaleidoscope that swallows
the turbulent veins of light inside me?

My Mother is Dying

I walk down the street
dank and cold, through soot,
past rows of tall,
narrow brownstone buildings,
homes with rows
of picture windows
that will drip tomorrow's rain
from the sky onto sidewalks,
into gutters and sewers
sunk beneath the street.

I greet my father on the stoop
by the gaslights
by the weathered front door,
and on down the hall to her room.

We watch her sleep,
suddenly thrashing,
rising straight and mindful,
lucidly clutching the end of day.

Her voice inflicts vitriol.
I feel for the first time
a deep-set frost in her eyes,
a fiercely penetrating glare
churning on the face
of a glazed woman
whom I'd not known well before.

There she sits, spilling word-syrup from her lips,
admitting, denying, unlocking her humor,
chanting rhythmically back and forth.

At dawn, her pain appears
in splotches, crass pleas
with silken pauses,
starts, moans, and grimaces.

My father stands alone,
juggling her craze, the sights and sounds
churning in the strange rectitude
of her head.

My father stands alone,
possessed of that vital civility
required to share
in the unsightly struggles of another.

Roused from a jealous peace,
we greet an endless train of friends
filled with pathos, who've come
to suffer through our smiles,
leave gifts of food, then leave.

In my maze, "truths" sometimes rise
as bastard children of irrevocable events,
for me to learn only *after*
that which has happened before.

And so it comes, *causa causans*,
to slowly chew her stale bread,
sip my last tea, pack my bag,

and out of that house
with the dire stone face,
gaslights lit like deep set eyes,
to wander the streets
wrung into thousands
of threadbare miles
of vacancy.

Letting Go

In this world, we dance in fidgets
across a boardroom floor.
Tiaras skip from queen to queen
in courteous games of fuzz
while kings advance
to conquer their foes
and their castles and trust.

Someday you'll leave your childhood,
lifting yourself from the icon
you've thought me to be—
rather, perhaps now a ghost,
a frozen totem taken
to his timely death.

You and I, we live in a book
of ancient history
with years of foreign flags
and faiths in folds of empty scabbards.
Each time a child is born,
I'm reminded of the dust
that I'll whisk from my sleeve
in the years ahead, and I'm glad.

Would it serve
to watch your father cry?

Maturity

I race to find myself before I die.
I leap between the lights and darks
of winding alleys, windblown streets,
anywhere, for a bit of respite
to soothe my delusional mind.

I search the city, red brick buildings,
crystal plazas, subways—
hail each stranger,
greet each faceless passerby
to keep from sinking
into drowning time.

Tonight, my room seems like a skeleton
stripped of human design and purpose.
I reach under my pillow for a turbine
to spur me on, for the pulse of an iron heart
to surge through my body.

I hide in the folds of my blanket.
My fantasies drive me to lose my mind.
But minds are cheap. I want to die for a cause
that makes me a hero, killed by a demon of stature,
where my death will be seen as a victory
and my likeness sewn to the mast of every ship
that cuts a tide to guide the world through life.

This thought is banal and shopworn and I'm ashamed
to talk so dramatically like most kids I know,

like Pokémon, moths shedding their caterpillar faces
for the great unknown, sucked into a lamp
and swatted to death.

Lonely Child on a Sandlot

I was born on a sandlot
roasting spuds with an odd old man

> tweed coat, chain fleece, warbled speech,
> brown-skin eyes with orange peels

pleading,

mother, mother, why do you hide each day,
sharing your bed with strange fishers?

> *I twirl to a frenzy, burning.*
> *not once, but twice and thrice.*
> *I've drunk my treasured delights*
> *in many dudes' crotch , my son.*

Your days are full of fawning roosters.
Their images streak
through the pupils of my eyes,
their flipping crests, ivory beaks,
ruffled shirtsleeves, trouser-bags,
down to their three-toed sneak-zips,
each phallus stuck with glue
to your tricks and twitches.

I've asked from you just one small smile
between your flake-filled rendezvous.
But your styling director
drives you to work, here and there,

in the sallow silk you wear
to please your jinns.

At the end, from the depths
of my futile pleas,
to whom can I weep?
To whom could I ever seep,
weeping for help in my struggle
to gain a bit of your frozen ground?

My old man tingles with blindness,
limbs ambushed by the Axe of Time,
still scrambling, scratching his absent mind
to fathom your thirsts.

But I think, in the end, his fingers
creep ever nearer to truth than regret

        tweed coat, chain fleece, warbled speech,
        brown-skin heart with orange love.

When I was a child

my father painted my eyes
strange colors.
Once in a weeks while,
when I slept, my lids would open.
My eyes would escape.
At dawn they'd return
as clean and innocently
unknowing as before.

Dreams are illusive.
They don't want to be real.
Sometimes they hide.
Sometimes they rouse me.
Sometimes it hurts
to think of their power
to reveal my pain.

When I was a child,
I spread sweets
among the friends
that lived in my crib.
I yearned to laugh,
but I often failed.

Try as one might,
one cannot always see
the air he breathes.

When I was older,
I fell to my knees
at my father's feet.

He'd never told me
I was not blind.
I groped through life
through his eyes,
for many-colored
sightless nights.

If only I'd felt dear to myself,
I might have understood
his love.
I might have redeemed him
if only I'd seen it
more clearly
or felt the dreams
that colored my heart.

Birthing

An infant longs to return to its mother's womb.
It wants to live immersed, without being born,
to spare them both pain and deprivation.

Some stories invent themselves.
Some find unknowns.
Told backward, they lose their surprise.
Told everywhere or not at all, their suspense.

Cacophony. With forceful invectives
and dogged release, we become the labor
that marks the way we emerge.

When the outer world appears,
I find my mother's ample breast.
I touch her sheen-brown skin,
her mellow voice, her smile.
I suckle.

Colostrum tastes like gall
yet holds a binding message.

We sing in verse.
We grow our sapphires together.

Erosion

I am the art of your erosion,
your speech quartered,
your space gathered,
thickets and thickets,
thorns and spikes,
castrati, eunuchs
that peer through your body
unlacing their fire
to shape your words,
perseverating blisters
that burst on the prongs
of your voice.

I am the mountebank
in the farthest corner
of your cloistered mind,
and you are my friend.

Coal

Dozens died in giant heaps,
in blizzards of dust,
worn lean by poverty,
hauling the bloodshot marrow
in their bones,
in their ton-weight boots,
driving steel
for the evening's
stone cup of soup
with hungry bread,
a slab of suet
and a slice of hell.

Now I've grown old.
My breath is gone.
I'll shrink into a grave
of mushrooms and mulch
and watch my wife
take her mourning days to market
to buy a peaceful life, without a thought
in the pocket of her scabs and patches,
without her man.

High Tea

Bonbons and flan soufflé,
tethered sliverness
on withered winery-buttered crumples.
From a gourmand tray across the table,
aperitifs for our guests,
kings and queens flaunting their gowns,
their sterling cravats and penguin-vests,
shiny medals crossing a floor with waltzing slogger
and a step or two from the past;

with hands and feet the shapes of elegance
pouring down a drain of azure blood,
blown to paradise in a field of tidbits,
having come together for a cup of tea.

Flowers

stood in a vase on a table
beneath the clock
on the freshly painted wall.
The clock stopped
just before
it might have struck six.

The room grew dim.
I could no longer see the time
or smell the paint.
Burdens fell
from our shoulders,
like shriveled steel.

When the time came
for us to leave and the pain
to leave our bodies,
tears dripped down
from the hands of the clock—
at almost the stroke of six.

Two flights up,

on a secluded street,
in the crags and creases of her bed,
she drowned herself in memorabilia.
Her sallow face told me
how near to death she must be.

She paused and stared seemingly forever
at her bare walls, searching,
not for cures or for solace,
but for a sign of meaning to her life.

I reached for the image of her god
that stood at her bedside.
I asked her to tell Him
what she wanted Him to know—
to ease her seething pain,
to forgive, to bless.
She wanted never
to die each day, alone.

In the waning light,
in the glow of dusk
in the rising of a starless night,
I asked her
what she'd want her God to say,
what she'd want him to tell her,
what she needed to hear.

Iron City

Homes were crowded,
company homes,
in a kingdom of fancy cars,
fancy labels and high heeled limbs;
homes on streets of Slavs,
indentured, baited,
English spoken poorly,
bending their backs
in constant prayer,
torn in the mill
by miniscule crystals of sand,
spicules worming
through their tiny sacs of air,
churning, turning north,
magnetic north,
so ripping at their lungs, crippling.

God should open His book of blasted pages
of burning fingers, lamplight hearths,
open hearths, torn men staring down
to greet the sintered floors
with hideous burns,
early unfit to stand the heat, red hot streams,
flaming ingots wrought into coins
into opulent pockets of gold.

If You Want to Know Who I Am

Mother fell from father's grave
into the arms of a brute.
She swept the dung from his anger,
wept in the toilet of his bed.
On our filthiest evening,
she passed into memory. He left.

Then came the homes, schools,
taunts, jails,
guards who'd just as soon
bash a brain or hump a boy
as smoke a joint.

In the morning, the sky lights up
the Birmingham Bridge.
I eat my bread to the smell of traffic.
I piss on the pylons, crap in the river.
My insides thrash from black pain.

If you want to know who I am,
I'm the Emperor of Japan.
You will bow as I pass.
I will toss you garlands,
wreaths of fortune, gifts of joy.

Years pass like geese in autumn,
wrecked on the rocks in the river—
Evenings? Stacks of sun downs.

Nights? Heaps of gall.
Frigid air streams through my home-like,
around my body.

Winds as old as I, raw, dry, shriveled,
blow away my story.
I cuddle my stray.

Daryl

School is a tiger.
My teacher? A hunchback
who stalks in the weeds—
half a face with an olive
for an eye, an earring,
thick lips and a mustache
that runs around his mouth
into a dirty gray beard.

The other half,
with a squinting eye,
spider-web sneers,
no mustache,
no beard at all.

And the third half,
a skull that burns,
bursts from the thrust
of the blade of a sword
to its broken head—

in a cage with a crazy mother,
crazy father, a circus of live-ins,

and that Civil War cannon
facing me down
across the schoolyard
from in front
of the courthouse, next door.

Parisian

What an empty bed must mean to a Parisian apartment,
one patched like a hat with cut flowers from a garden
lain against the window of a fog,
staked along the banks of the Seine.

She wore her hairpiece long and straight
to match her putty-face and the heavy tint
on her cheeks, lilting out
along the shadowed banks of the Seine.

She whimpered at his husky mane,
wrapped his fingers around her breasts.
Her nails trawled deep
beneath the fleshy crust
of the nape of his neck,
on the silent banks of the Seine.

He stripped her down, spread her thin,
buttered her with craving
and thrust her through the night.

He dragged her putty-face
to her room and over her blue-green spread.
A curtain hung from the right hand corner
of the bedroom window,
dancing in the dancing breeze.
He said his usual prayer and moved on,
as did morning,
that bore the poxes of rain
that covered the surface of the Seine.

Act III

You've become my mirror, distorting my shape,
exposing my striae, twisting me
into corsets and cramped silhouettes.

Your smile, in small doses of morphine happiness,
squeezes through my insides, transforming my features

into tremulous choreographs with steps and poses
befitting a whore. Pimp and whore.

I see waxen fruit in a bowl on a table,
fermenting with the clock, with the chimes of a clock
grown old and infirm as they drop their time to the floor.

And here we sit, transparent on our tawdry stage,
devoured by a montage of hungry words.

No heroes, no villains, no interlopers, no time,
we sweat under stale comic lines and soliloquies,

with nothing to distinguish our drama
but the pith of our smothering love.

Kewpie doll and puppeteer,
we limp across a desert stage,
strangled by tears, as the curtain drops

and the theater slowly comes alive,
and the audience sits silent in their seats.

Emily

My hand leans
between your breasts
and presses lightly–
your heart. Encased
in bellows
with their rush
of thin air–
your lungs.

Music from a seraphim,
sings restrained,
slow then fast then slow,
broken by flutters.
Ripples with sudden thumps
with gasps and drubs,
yield to their pause.

The Heap of a Man

I never grasped the force of his smile,
of the scar that streaked down his face,
his glare of pig iron and gravel, his crust.

He lived like a Buddha, cheeks starched,
thick lips, eyes hung down
from the weight of his woolen brows,
paunch as firm as his joy of barley rot
and whiskey sludge.

Streams of tar rolled
through the trenches in his lungs.
His mien grew bent to the curve of his back,
to the shape of his rocker,
to his hairy arms and legs and, in the end,
to his forehead, in cold sweaty beads.

Tinted windows chill.
My mother loosens her hair.
The pulpit burns with stoic words,
mighty words, wrinkled words
about a cask of years
about the heap of a man..

In a Charitable Manner of Speaking,

we share a bed
divided by the ways
we keep our secrets smoldering,
subtle plots of intrigue,
piqued-playful, pristine
in our toadstool garden of verses.

We vault to the rooftop in cycles
of wishing and waning,
and nursing and prepping
our children to seek
their own caverns
in which they can hide
when we joust.

My love,
our years have crumbled,
we, extinct.
Riddles no longer
have reason to charm us.
They died in our sleep.

Yet, by tacit agreement,
we cling to endure our pain,
to spare us the cost of our grief,
the expense of drowning
in bursts of sorrow and loneliness.

My Dream

pours from a crucible
into a cask,
seething deep brown-green—
annealing, cooling homologous
and hard, tenacious, astir, afoot,
stealing into my house
and up the circular stairs,
through the doorway
and across the room,
to kneel beside the portrait
of my beautiful wife,
as I knew her long ago.

Helplessness

I wish I could whisk a pile of figurines
or some other porcelain objects

in a long swipe across my mantle,
crashing them on the floor.

Instead, I rock back and forth,
pounding my fist against a book.

I open to a story, roam through the words
mindlessly searching for relief.

I roll with the giant waves in a picture
of an angry sea, spiked on cliffs

that line its shore, trapped in the oily slick
spread from the bellies
                of foundered ships.

Eventide

Windows blew out, curtains shredded.
Thunderclaps glazed us in bursts
that burned the city to a fossil, to gall and cinders.

I carved your name on the splintered bridge,
the rotting bench in the garden.
I found your grave. I washed your stone with care
to protect the past from oblivion,
the future from the scourge.

We Grow Up

It's one thing to search
amongst the barren streets,
quite another to find nothing
but lonely tropes within myself.

I reek of seclusion of the kind
I learned as a child;
the dread I feel in crowds,
when noise masquerades
as a pretext for virtue.

I've searched for majesty
in what I've just said,
but can't find it—
only a paper thin feeling
of failure that should have burned me
to cinders on the road back home.

Lips Receiving Phallus

A tulip circles
in a pleasant breeze

that dances her
far across a room

carried back
by a feisty wind
to an aura

in which a chicken molts
sucking the instant
to lodge in her bed

in the luscious form
of a gentleman

This poem was meant to capture an undulating progression
of movement (by the tempi and line breaks) that leads
to the motif, *aura*, which then expands into the genital symbol
of a man.

Self-Portrait

If there were a flower
in the vase
by the pot
    slowly steeped
        in its cozy
on the table
in the garret
of this desolate
man always posed
    in self-portraits,

one that throws back his pain
to his mirror,
    primed to speak
        each day from the lingering
        wounds of his youth,

if there were at least a pair of boots
and gloves to protect him
 from despair—

but he sees no hues or forms
 and I cannot direct him
 to where they might be found.

He would not
  know my name
    or search my mind

or believe he could ever rise
from his useless noise.

Yet I would press this flower
             between the pages of a poem
                    and give him a gift
                          he would have to endure.

In a Darkened Room

There are many ways
to hide in a darkened room.
When I'm with you, I search
the person I think I ought to want to be.
I shrink to approximations
behind an armor-papered wall.

My senses want to slip away.
But I'm caught, dissolved
in your stream of confetti—
my trial for having tried
to leave at all.

Water, the shape of a kiss,
runs between our sheets.
Then there is nothing left
but the shape of a tear,
deformed to a splat
across my state of mind.

I drink mirages to preserve them,
shrunk to a single mote,
packaged in a sound that brings me peace.

When I'm with you,
I stand rigid, at the foot of Elysium,
blazing with passion to have you once more.
I cross through the dark, against traffic
in the corner of the room.

I was born

with many thoughts and feelings
written on my face.
I've tried to understand them
by their meanings
and by those I've stealthily
hidden from each other's view.
I've waited for each
to reenact its drama.
But, in my defense,
I'd erased them all.

History of the World

He is bald with a long cigar.
Upright pianos play hymns.
Words might find you sleeping.
Smoke, muddy.

Shopping baskets fill with candy.
Children tease their pets
and the sermon is good.

He is bereft with his brown cigar,
bald head on his desk,
crying aloud for antiquity
which is all he remembers
learning to do.

Our Father

His black felt hat casts a shadow
on his eyes.
His brows point down
to his black bearded chin.
His hands wave him on through the air.
His trailing black coat, his dangling legs,
pitch him, like a kite, still higher.
We should look up to this man
and give thanks
for his remarkable feat.

The Mob

Henchmen of disfigured causes
without names on their faces,
roused by invidious masters
to drive their power, their rage—

I'd tripped on a pot of anonymous men
who lean on bluster to kindle their *truths*.

I covered my ears with the palms of my hands.
That helped.

I folded my eyes beneath my lids,
hid my thoughts in filigree, choked them,
strangled their meanings.
I covered my lips, shrank my voice,
squeezed it tight.

I felt myself slip like a toady,
a prickly fish,
barb of a hook lodged in its gills.
I swam in a frenzy,
in the style of the moment,
with the flow of the mob.

Parade

Blaring bells of tubas.
Batons twirl,
parade through the streets
in a fanfarade that bulges
with cheers.

And fancy shops?
Novel scented
leather-woolen fruits
and cocktails leak
from under their doors,
from out their picture windows
onto sidewalks
that burn their lamps
that line the curbs
with trees that silently bend
to the breezes of springtime.

A swashing candy floss
of sounds flies over the crowd.
A hansom, then a dray,
a wagon filled with pensioners
scruff on their lips,
swilling their brew,
this dying breed of revelers—
laughter, rollicking
down the streets,
up into the beds of lovers
at the height of their afternoon,
oblivious to the laughter
in the street below.

The Last Hurrah

Tuesday follows Monday.
Wednesday disappears
from the face of the Earth,

the intercession of obscurity
in the name of peace.

Most of me lives in the words
of my friends, a piece of me
in those photos on the shelf,
least, in my dwindling mind.

And I've come to tell you,
I'm perfectly confused.
I can't understand a word
you've said.

Soon I'll run like soiled water
down the drain of a sink
of dirty dishes,
shouting invectives,
riding on a wind
of vanishing footprints
to the shrine of a vengeful God.

There is Pity in the House

How can I tell you of hardship?
Canons that gnash, shining in the dark,
changing dark to dark light
to lightning dark, with claps of clouds
bumping head-on-head
in a windowless sky, in a broth
that should never have existed?

Infants picked at random,
transients, with no eyes to cry
or close to open?

Rag dolls pulled from ragged
breasts of mothers?

And what is in a tear?
One part glory, another damnation,
demise, candy statues,
gold scrubbed with pomade
as if it were skin,
black and brown, children fleeced,
flushed down drains
by laws that rip them
to custard sweet cookies
that make us laugh ourselves to death?

What is in a tear?
A half-mast flag salutes in a language
mourning truth.

An impacted bowel bursts with hubris,
ripe for its grisly stories to tell.

We watch from the temper of a law
on a street where people are considered
nothing more
than legends forcing their ways
through unwritten books,
where loneliness is a but a father
drawn on a rack to writhe
in a desperate afterlife.

There is pity in the house.
I tell you, naked pity.

I tell you there must be a certain pity
that walks the courtyard of hell
when we look on, helplessly joyful,
crawling through our pseudo days.
Hardship is so absent, that we might
not miss it at all or remain silent
with shame for the love we have lost
to ourselves.

In a Cup of Tea

This is my way of saying
my silence,

neither living nor dying,
but holding my speech,
fending off those portions
of people,

bitter perhaps, that might never know
what they've wanted to know,
what they've dreamed
of becoming.

You ask why now
I dwell in the heart
of foibles?

What's left
to the dignity of desire?
Is there speech? Erudition?

Must one have credentials
to grind the past to sand?
To remember one's reach
for each other's private
tender-living bodies?
To discover in the shower
the cog that wheels
a naked mind?

Silence is the economical way
to say everything at once.

Dormancy bleeds me dry
onto empty pages
of everyman's hobbling
in a way as to render
what I'd stutter to say
drowned in the shuffle
of repetitive verbal gimp,
hidden in the useless shield
of a somber (somber or not) thirst
for a rain-soaked stroll
to a street-side cafe, my dear,
to a spoon in a cup of hot tea
or a cup of no tea at all.

Conformity

I see my self pasted to my bed
in which I sink
one degree at a time,
driven by each turbulent dream.

I've danced among fairies
assuring my comfort,
cherubs, in a ménage
that shadowed my pleasures,
that sucked up the frights
of my childhood.

But childhood, my friend,
cannot see into the future.
And denial will not listen,
only laugh
and grow greater and stronger,
closer, more endearing,
strangling by its grace and demure,
by its conformity to my days.

Fractals

I want to give you the ocean
but it is too heavy to carry.
Coastlines will erode to sand,
coalesce into slurries.
Salt will run with the rain
that will bring down the sky
with its weightiness.

Cold will want to eat the sun.
The Earth, to survive,
will need to change its shape,
a cube or a cone.
And you'll look different,
more sanguine than before.

You'll feel stronger,
think in floods of crystals
of snow that fly with the air,
as mists into winds
that capture your sensibilities.

At the end of your life,
you'll have forgiven the past.
You'll wonder what you were like
before you left it behind,
before you found
whom you actually came to be.

Silence

I speak to the silence with which I've lived—
a world full of silence, cooked and caked,
sieved through my fingers,
caught in a cage of symbols that stick
to one's tongue like knots of garlic and guile.

My name is Cremona. I've slept each night
with the seasons of the Earth.
I've danced nude in a scarf, a howling dervish
around the neck of a vigil,
silently, but ever so shiny and bright,
so evanescent in the life of a moon,
that disappears, that dies each morning,
mute, without a sound.

Madonna

Have I told you of the millions of shades of green,
brown and yellow leaves that crawled across the road,

or of the kudzu that climbed trees in towering cascades
to smother them with lush,
or of the nearby stream, dissolved in the tendrils
of a thirsty wind,

of the slick speed that wiped the road,
the fatal curves, that careened me into a ditch?

Have I told you that I lay last night with a woman
who stroked me to sleep, who made me forget to wince,
forget the strangled trees and my snaking
through the gorge?

Have I told you of her bosom
and the beads she wore around her neck?

Thank the Hallows

for the way he spreads himself
across the valley
in his long black robe and steed,
as he catches the poor, as he rides one
to glory in Hell.

Kill him. Kill him, I say.
But no one hears the speed
with which he crosses
the Stykes,
no telling what else
is not heard
in our sun striped wild,
in our tumult of joy.

Trollop

Here you are, sitting beside me,
spine shone through your blouse,
eyebrows fierce, lips abundant,
soft, melancholic,

waiting in a lobby
for the matron to come,
both of us frightened,
singing under our breaths,
for distraction, speaking bubbles,
watching them fly above the city,
burst amongst sun strokes,
waiting for the call.

Lovers

I don't know whether it will make sense to you,
whether you'll see that hidden in our footsteps,

in the lining of our clothes,
there is an invisible pain,

a pain that rises above the flesh and touch,
not as invective, affliction,

but as a filament with a tiny voice
that whispers, "fear",

and a wanting eye, with a glaze
that watches our fear contort

as it burrow within us.
Must we flee, a pair of women

who have reached for ourselves
above the thunder of a troubled world?

Can you know how much it matters
for me to write these lines?

To pour myself into a story
that bulges from the sheer force

of its foreboding? For me to waken
to a New Year's day

amongst a crowd of hostile revelers,
when I ask for you, and you to cry?

Hunger

Each night, I cry. My tears leak
through a hole my sleep,
soaking me, drop by drop,
drowning me
deep in my spongy bed,
my breasts too small
to nurture my child.

I'll heal my wounds a bit
from time to time.
But I can't mend
the rage in the gut
of the genie I harbor.
I can't keep his ghost
from gnawing me.

I swam for years
through the eyes of my father.
He follows me still,
a ghost with the cunning
of a shark,
as if I were but bait
for a god who reigned
by the skill
of his organs of love,
to sire my son, a pearl
in the carapace of grief.

Fetish

He found a niche
in the corner of his room.
For hours he lay,
wrapped around his arms
and legs and body.

He swaddled his fetish
in finely sewn quirks.

Furors plowed through him.
Streets and valleys
filled with faceless crowds
that grew and grew
in vast proportions.

Helpless to stop their advance,
he kneeled alone inside
his infant state of mind,
covering his head
like a dybbuk that hides
from the image of god.

He flooded his sleep
with nightmares,
pleading to die,
to free him from the years
that had taught him
the compulsions

that have shaped his seclusion,
his dungeon,
with faceless rituals—
once discovered, found out,
derided, each day
more lethal than the day before.

On the Face of the Sea

I'm falling inward,
failing within, imploding
in the throes of a seizure,
trembling, with jarring spells,
years sailing past each breath.

Everywhere draws near.
Words refuse.
Tyrants in my mind
unravel, pruning my senses,
compelling me to whip
shadow-lesions into scars,
taut, grotesque,
like gargoyles spewing rain
from the mouths of cathedrals
to nourish the earth
in the middle of the night.

I cannot move, frigid,
with the helplessness
of a newborn
caught in the womb
on the eve of its mothers
dearest moments.

Can I have perished,
full of leaves,
crisp for Autumn's denuding,
caught in bursts

from the sun, auroras,
prisms in the starry night?
Then everything goes black,
disrupted.

I am not deluding myself
or crushing myself,
or thieving, robbing,
fugitive from some rife law,
without a trace or an imprint,
molten in the body
of a kiln that glazes me
into an artifact.

I have not killed anyone
I might wish dead,
not a specter dancing before me,
shouting into my ears,
pursuing me running,
flying through the galaxies
crying my name
until I'm speared by some god,
sent to hell, buried, forgotten,
convulsing
through the story of my life.

Why am I wandering
like an evil angel
disguised as an omen,
to burn in the underglades
until I repent?

Teach me now,
in your most gracious way,
how to thwart the anguish
of a bastard child
who must scatter his name
on the face of the sea
to reclaim his drowning soul.

Message from the Underworld

The world is filled with enemies.

We lift ourselves to the surface of whirling,

    whirling
pellets
        of blood,

    past envelopes
of dulcet clouds—we,

who shout into the stratosphere
    to the pinnacle of what was, was—is,

supremacy in façades—

    half gods   half goddesses,

powers, driven by the many

    turning forces   of turning,

        inevitably,

shaping their own

        shapes!

Enjoy what has ever

been   termed enjoyment—

drawing   claques,
                        for a synthesis

from the middle of the past,
                        having cared

                much about little—
marching to the unity of chaos.
                A bitter
peace of mind,
                        that marches
to the tempo of the crises.

Insects

perched on bandwagons spew their seeds
of sweet acid,

        their peaches,   hiding their pits.

Dragons fly brilliant fright
around entirely living,

        saturating rooms,
saturating walls,

ceilings   floors,   eventually
dragging down the peace,

eventually to the ground,
                        melting its face,
killing the fractures
from which it comes screaming,

grown into nations
of fractures,   unrest, thrust
    inside blinding
            cloaks of sweetness,

driving towards collapse,
the exhilarated rush to extinction.

Shame on the ingenuity of tears

and reconciliation,   traversing
      us, laughing at the doorstep of hell,

with our speeches in floated air,
too bloated,
too sweet,
too thick,
too cruel,
too broad an expanse,
for us to avoid their briers—

grinding machines
play with the same kinds of toys;

ambiguities, muddled language,
       muddled   with messages

rushing us to the rush of the apocalypse,

numbers of steeds of doom,

(eight, nine, ten, seven six, who knows)—

       even with horsemen, henched,

              even non-sexuals, eunuchs

that devised the witch-hawks,

the white-light dark-sky gospels

meant

       to prevent the crowd from divesting.

Harsh forms, we, who call ourselves *friend,*
for salvation,
       sleeping on our bitter pits—

"and be ye mute and glad each day
                     you ratchet round
       false fires

touting false Freedom,
extinguished by your death."

On a Turn in the Bend of the Road

I found the blue-green eyes of a boy,
lying on his back, lips and cheeks,
face sprawled across the sky,
wrapped in snow.

I searched his eyes for life.
A little life? A lot? Its price?
Tallied? Bought with silver?
Bought with solid gold?
Stoic gold? Precious? Brilliant?
Worthy and muscular
golden slabs of pyrite,
pure, with vivid hues?

I closed the boy's olive drab lids,
scarlet ribbons trickling down
his temples into a field
of shriveled pain.

A letter in his vest pocket,
bloodshot, tattered,
spoke of violins from Cremona
crossing the Po to drench us
in some lavender kind of peace,
some beautiful kind of lavender peace.

Chinese Figurine

Touch the wind. Now it is yours,
woman with deep set eyes
draped beneath your ruffled hair
(grown longer now than ever before).

A beautiful day, bronzed,
from behind a Chinese figurine,
watches us,
wrapped in the ways of waltzing rhythms,
telling us to comb the snow,
so softly falling into our minds,
in their quarter inch of an instant
of an eye, of a window picture
with the fountain in the park.
That is yours.

My Son

Light splits the shadows
that cross your face.
It tells me who you are.

Otherwise you would escape me
as the night would want you to do,
as it speaks in a language
of faults and foibles,
as I lie here
hoping you will wake
and light the light
so you can see my face
and my glimmer, and cry.

Our window shows a drama,
a scene with actors
that work through a script
that was written to please,

and lilacs, their faithful scent
that finds its way
through the house—
when we let it in.

But the fence reminds me
to think of things to come..

The gate squeaks prophetically
when it's opened—

hesitatingly, slowly,
then closes on a latch
that speaks finality
up the path to our front door,
and into our worried beds.

The postman brings a letter—
too late.

Questions

I'm trying to find the instant
apart from all others that lived before,
echoes of speeches, wild prayers,
music in flashes of light,
purchased light, jeweled light
to carry in my pocket.

Those that live tomorrow
will take me with them,
atonal seasons, hell and virgins,
innocence and the reaper
carving gravestones precisely
where my aspirations lie.

My instant today will fade
on the next page,
woven into forgoing goodbyes.

I try to grasp enduring oaths
and vows, commands and biddings—

but I'm whirling
in the confusion
of what you've just said
and the way you said it.

Then, only in doubts
might I understand what you mean
and I can't.

Who are you?
For what am I searching?
For what have I died all my life?

I doubt if I'll ever be able
to take the chance to find the instant
to grasp the purpose
for which I was born.

The Day I Came to Realize

that words have feelings,
I discovered that not all words
are equal.

Bosch tried to save us
from our proclivities.
He laid out our strong
and weak words,
our mirror images,
on a canvas,
and asked us to agree.
We refused.
We took his strokes
for belittlement,
raised our flags,
and recoiled. No one
bought his bread.

Sometimes I feel abandoned
as when strong rivers spring
from pious ponds.
I want to purge myself
of the flag I've worn
on my breastplate.

But without an identity,
how can I recognize the doorstep
on which I was born?
How can I love coming home

to a house that burned down
soon after I learned to speak,
and swept all words away.

422

We distinguish ourselves by distilling those of others,
each of us with two-sided heads and torsos and
sashes and swords, advancing a bit in the
morning, retreating into an indigent cloud
that passes overhead, embracing our-
selves with the places we'd wished
to have been and the station
to which we would wish to
have risen, laughing
through the glass
that has lost us
our vantage
point,
our content.

Dream Walk

Her outstretched arm cuts
to the left a
slowly
circling
windmill swath
through the fog. Her other
arm, fist stretched
taut in front,
leads
her unswerving
shoulder,
head
and neck,
her staunch body forward
in resolute steps.
A specter tugs
at the circling arm,
shredding her gown,
wrapping
itself around her,
still unable to
thwart
the force
of her belonging.

Nature

I have had in mind
not to describe nature
but to step back into it –
not to carry the burden
of a lens by which simile
becomes objets d' art
but to walk through night-lit
streets and lightning arcs
allotted me,
onto wharves and into unplowed
clouds as part
of their goings on –

not to bake brave precepts
in gold leaf but to share them
at the table in the unpredictable
taste of spleen soup,
while somehow searching
the silent faces around for ways
to capture my feelings
so specifically that they cannot
be dismissed, so generally
that their presence in others
cannot be denied,
yet so unlike both
as to discover the very people
I've seen so many times before.

Traveling North

Love
sprouts from lichen on the north
side of a tree, moss
in the shade

by a lily pond.
Green is the color
of devotion, scrubbed
by night

three
or four times, kneeling,
dragged, now dressed
in elegance.

And I learn
to speak slowly, carefully
feeling my name,
then yours.

And we build
a stalk of cracked corn.
And I take you
through the smoky light,

and we live,
half curled

and half
undressed, washed in soapy
water, hung
to dry.

Dyula

We laughed. We shaped the ways
we'd laugh,
pouring cream amongst the glories,

You would say*; three edges to one's*
smiles,
so one might touch all the faces
that live in the orchard.

Renoir crossed his legs in poverty
while he painted his beauties.

Rodin sculpted Rilke's Duino,
of course,

from his whispers
to his bronze language of gestures.

And I, both poor and mute, I've wanted to speak,
to tell them all of all of our days denied,

lost proofs, vanished souvenirs, of our nuances, minute
skews of speech,
dissolved in the daily bursts of familiar white noise.

I might have done so, if not for the day
you fell from the swing and I caught you and you cried.

But you were simply too young and chilled
to know what I meant.
And the ground was so slushy wet.

Atonement

Past gaseous light,
to the granite of an antediluvian wall,
figures came slowly, wholly
together into focus,
for a view through the eyes
of the miniscule
at the throne of a vascular God.

With twilight near, we lit candles.
Voices wept as angels sang,
twisted threads of string,
threaded twine unstrung,
sweet silt of night.

Then the long ram blast of a horn.
Three, then nine more cries
for the paupers and penitence.

Falling from the brow of a cellist,
murmurings, at first,
grew to heaves and thrusts,
tangled knots on a vine
vibrating valiantly into solid air—
lamentations drawn across the body
and over the muted bridge to a quietude
where a scroll swung free with its gentle words.
And we sang.

Why do you sing your confessions with joy? *
We whispered back and the winds
swung from stars hard as gems,
ripe with our affection.

* Baal Shem Tov

Red Fox

Red fox runs
  a tea cup in his hair

Beetles trample drying grapes
  windmills slice the country air

River by my window sill
  walks with pride 'mongst apple trees

Words so gently spoken here
  go flying with the rain.

In Search

I find my way in search
through darkened rooms

laced by dark windows or
where the windows

ought to be or
used to be or

where painted sea oats
simulate the outdoors
in place of portals or

where footsteps climb
to track me down

where I ought to be or
where my flagellant images

drive me or
where I've driven my mind

into caves and blow holes
hidden wandering

through relics,
now prostrate in the dark
lain on the foggy bottom
ready for sleep.

Me

I feel to sing in sounds
the size of mammoth stones,
conglomerate blues and grays
with seams of iron wine,
welded by the force of my belonging,
clothed in heather, thrumming,
in my flight high above the tree line,
as to drift toward the ceiling of the sky.

Meandering

I live over there
on that rusted
railroad bridge
that walks on stilts,
on its dragging pylons
up and down the river,
losing me in and out
of the wildlife, night life
that lights its ons and offs
beneath the wet
that bathes the crusted
valley in slithers,
that butt and bend
their streams around
the mossy rocks
that guard the pools
of minnows
from the surge
of the force
of the mountain,
each day.

The Peddler

Gimping foot,   dra-g-gg
the next   perching
on the heap   on my
shoulders   keep astride
my shifting burden   sack
slung back   neck
                    thrust forward
step a
            slo-o-ow   tr-o-d
down the rutty pot-hole road

With the burden trickling down
Hep it up Up higher Harder
Hoist   the heavy bulge
Heft it Ho!

Salt and silt   cake up
my eyelids   Forehead drips
the taste of
brine   down
    to the cleft in my
    stubble-chin

From my rambling lips
bing words
hawk the burdens
        in my sack

On sale With a shifty shrill

Buy my answers!
Buy them all!

Purchase two for the
lovely price of a ......
Take   a few   or a bunch
for special seasons
Take plenty!
And many!
Keep your wretched purses.
take them aaalllllllllllll !

My throat whispers   once
          again
  not parched, not frenzied,
Please   good people
take my torment
     Let me grope.

Let me shuffle   walk alone
       threadbare feet
          fetid soul

gimping
              dre-g-gg
the next
slowly   shifting   raise my arms
to split my rocks
       to probe their totems

burst my heart
     to   find a soul
inside   before I die

Step a
      slo-o-ow trod
            down the rutty pot-hole road

Good-bye

Good-bye

Girl With Auburn Hair

I

Grief let down her auburn hair.
She wept alone in the arms
of the oaken chair
on the stand near the flag
by the bench and the gavel
in the giant hand
of a giant black robe,
in the face of anonymous pews
that faced the honorable seal
struck there on the wall,
skewed by blades of amber light
thrust through the keyhole
of the court, a sinking cathedral
surrounded by smoldering dunes,
where silence is scorn,
where captives of tragedy
come to mourn.

She sat there alone,
folding herself into sparkling flickers
that streaked through the sky
to the lair of her Mandarin Dragon,
uncoiling its rice paper crepe,
cavorting, chuckling, snorting
through its hokey mouthpiece,
floating down beside the child

to clear the sweat from her temples,
to guide her breath, her frozen words
that strained to reach her lips,
that lapsed instead into shafts and bogs
that lined the catacombs deep inside her chest.

    II

Fright unfolded her carnival twilight
of crystal faith, conjured her mythical
Gypsy Queen of Spades,
Mistress of Cause and Blame,
Mother to All,
who gently strokes small girls
with auburn hair,
flown from their beds to come
and wish to die,
their fractured fathers crawling,
wrenching, thrusting, mauling
the kin of their souls.

"Done!" Swallowed and spent.
She drowned her shame
against her pillow.
He swaggered to his bed
while mother drew deep sleep
with blindfold eyes,
with deafened ears,
perfumed by the pumice
engraved in the pendent that hung
by a chain round her neck,
lending her the courage to dream
nothing but sweetness and joy.

Pristine psalms prevailed.
Morning appeared
from the boughs of a hemlock.
Scenes grew dim in dawn's raw light
as memory forgets its assailants.

III

From my house,
from the terrace of my chamber,
on the crest of compassion,
I looked down
on the busy streets below.
I watched the runaway daughter
in her hide and seek.

I saw her sift through a sidewalk
crowd of elbow-hips, through nations
of shining steel and glass on rubber tubes,
parked in perfect rows, in torqued suspense,
these sleeping hounds that strain their tether,
poised to suddenly wake, start engines,
blow horns and lunge home.

Plucked like a penny from a basement trough
beneath a sidewalk, she was carefully lifted
then suddenly snatched, placed in a pocket
of the law, and carried to court.

Matrons swept her inward and up
through galleries of gaping staunch old men

forever framed on the wall. She entered the drama,
crossing the "stage" and into the arms
of the old oak chair in its silently moaning ecstasy.

IV

(Travesty Law, a case in point in the byways
of a runaway Prudent Juris)

"All rise. Hear yeee, here in the Court of Torts!"
The magistrate bent his jowls, galumphed his gavel,
his nodded assent.

With the drone of a wasp, the father spread his wings,
drew bead and pressed, launching his prattle through the air,
stinging his "Runaway daughter", here and there, again, again.

Her heart ripped through her breast. She stumbled mute.

"More! Encore!" Frescos lifted from the walls, delightedly frenzied,
dancing, chanting their favorite tunes to the whine of his engine.

His toga flapped behind his gnathic grin. His chariot gathered speed
dusting piety up and down the aisles, touching every shoulder in
every seat
with his incantations, intonations, incarnations, abjurations,
a prithee of righteousness wrapped in the warp and weft of his
discourse,

No-good-lying-whore-of-a-runaway daughter!
Yes, I've-sadly-finally-said-it-and-I'm...
worry... ingrate... suffer...

With the whisper of a moth, he burrowed his way
through the paper thin walls of his "wholesome home".
In a fulsome drone, in a studied, hesitant slither,
he smiled with his teeth in his eyes,
with their gleam of demeaning charisma.
Then he shrank into his hole in the sod.

Mother's pupils dilated rage. Her torment burst into flames,

> *Amen, Daddy, Amen!*
> *Tell her to leave you be...*
> *For the devil's in her bed.*
> *Daddy, Daddy,*
> *come back to me,*
> *back where you belong ...*
> *Amen, Daddy, tell them, 'Amen!'*
> *For once, just for once...*
> *Pleasssssssse?   Just for meeeeeeeeeeeeeeee?*

Pathos welled from the glands in her eyes, leaking down
to her tongue in blithering puddles of prose
that gouged deep trenches in each of the girl's twelve short years,
tangling in the matted disarray of her auburn hair.

Her heart ripped through her dress, dripping as it tumbled as it beat.

V

Licking his truffles from the bones of his chops,
the judge rested for lunch with his fanciful bailiff (a venerable caliph),
the pro-sexecuter, defender-imputer,
the dichter-the-doctor, the richter-the-rector,

solicitors, voyeurs, inveigling boyars,
all out to lunch, on a cakewalk of cordials and scrunch.
The menu was stacked.
But the docket was lean. The pickings came mean,
munching pyrite that passed for gold
seared with charcoal to taste very old.

And this afternoon's venue had nothing
for sweets, so the bailiff was frightfully rude:

Order! Order! Stand up...Step down!
Case number two-seven-ten.
Do you swear? And forbear?
State your name, your game,
your claim to fame.
Wattav Ye Dun Furmee Lately?

Came the magistrate's judgment in trite singsong swill,
Dearly beloved, good friends of goodtwill,
the hour is late, the discourse, grand.
I am happy to say joyous things
on this day to the pretty young wench
on the stand

(Rio Grande, monkey gland, saraband, second-hand).

Go, little miss. Go succor your dad.
I've a heaven-bound wish for your bliss"

(pustuliss, gangreniss).

And I preach you, beseech you,
to reach you and teach you that

HOME IS SWEET HOME –
a message of clear benefice

(blubberniss, polydiss, mediocre rancorfiss).

You must thank the light-tainted reign of the court
.... of the court ...
with a toast to its clemency,

(wrought and sought and bought by green paper dumplings
dropped from a secret place through secret space
into a well known laundering pot).

VI

Her heart
paused,
plunged down
the front of her dress,
burst,
splashing her legs,
rippling red at her feet
as it reeled in pain
and died.

Her empty eyes
and aching neck
and limbs and back
embraced the worn
old chair. Her auburn hair
streamed softly
in the waning window light.

Dragon and Gypsy
faded in amber tones.
They wandered out
from the empty pews,
up over steeples
and over the dunes,
through parks and lots,
to rest in gutted schools
where nothing
had been gleaned,
in rooms without desks,
without blackboards,
black with the black
of night, the night

so full of the far away
horns of the homebound,
venting their
wrath on the roads,
on their ways to their homes.

The Portuguese *

I catch the squall
against the mizzen.
Watch him trip
his hurdy-gurdy tunes
inside his dory singing,
feesh, to my feesh,
grinding hurdy-gurdy,
feesh, leetle ones.

Toss your wreaths
from the headlands
on Gloucester's cliffs
to the trailing tide
of the Portuguese,

and sing, sank down
with the breakers,
sank down, by God, he did!

And my eyes
run with sorrow
as the taste of silt,
with his song
to hiss feesh in the sea.

* inspired by Captains Curageous
by Rudyard Kipling, 1897.

In the Ring *

Under the sizzling lights,
the pugilists dance
catch the shrieks
of the ringside butcher-birds
drooling through their beaks,
gorged on popcorn,
raw meat and happy times,
smoothing the draw
on their cigarillios.

Cubic jaws
pummeled knuckles.
Bulging flexed hulks doubled
on the ropes, repelled,
then doubled once more,
stung on their styptic lips,
lids blotched purple,
rage squelching the roar
of their pain. Then one dull thud.
No chipping, feinting,
no slap or two or three swipes,
no sidewinders, but a single
punch to a dumbstruck bull's eye
and Blam – a requiem.
A soft dull thud unraveling
brains down the aisle
in white spiral chains, the spirit
of the moment soaring

with psychedelic cheers that echo
to the count of ten.

* Inspired by "Tyson tri-trump-phant",
1980, gouache on paper by Red Grooms

Mr. Universe*

Perfect rows of teeth
light up his window smile,
rounded by the caverns
etched in his tan
oily cheeks,
his plastered yellow
head of hair, cuboid jaw,
and bull neck
built
on massive shoulders,
pectoral monoliths,
right wrist clutched
by his left hand,
right fist clenched tight
to "pop" the muscles
in his arm.

With a lively step,
Mr. Universe makes
his first debut
amidst a flurry
of well deserved cheers
from a tele-view throng
whose impeccable taste
has been ceremoniously
sanctioned by the judge.
His second debut
will take place..........

* From the art of Red Grooms

Cortland Alley *

Have you not seen
the street sign
and the big red truck
crashing out
from that wall named "Garage,"
a fat policeman
and a green thief
around a hydrant
soaked in dog piss,
past a bleak
lady in yellow hose,
Hing Lung bean sprouts,
fire escapes
and clothes lines,
muggings in the shadow,
and a teamster's day
in four or five dimensions, loading his van,
his pin ups
on the warehouse wall,
chanting,
Come to me, baby?

* From the art of Red Grooms

Affection

Have you ever walked through the woods?
Taken notice of a fat robin, chirping,
flying frantically over your head?
Have you found before long a second robin,
less colorful than the first, also teasing
and dodging you through the brush?
Have you imagined that these birds,
having flown more than once together,
might be coaxing you away from their nest?
Have you wondered where the nest
and the eggs might be?
Have you wondered about how very much
these robins must be loved by each other?
Have you let them lead you on?
Then, have you batted at the blue jay
come swooping down to find the eggs,
determined to chase it away.

At The Big Game *

Fifty thousand hot dogs
spread their mustard
down the aisles,
with Coke lakes
and straw people
gaping at the goal
posts as they merge,
float toward each other,
toward the center of the field,
orange and blue teams
each squeezing
to make touch downs
in end zones placed
on the fifty yard line,
to win-win-win
all day, to win.

But also to riff
with blasts
of trumpets
and cymbals
and big bass drums,
with wild cheers
from orange and blue
pleated skirt leaders
who whoop the crowd
to a frenzied
"Ra-Ra-Ra,"
"Sis-Boom-Ba!"

in quest of a living cause,
an enduring faith,
an anthem, a patriotic
tour de force in the form
of helmets and cleated shoes.

* From the art of Red Grooms

Lord Byron and His Friends

From my pedestal in the park,
I see doting love ride by
in carriages, and streams
of two-wheeled
cycling tourmalines.
Then there's the tramp!
His long shoes flap
in his pygmy shuffle
with his duck-walk cane
and the twirl of his mustache
as he turns to twinkle
the Dames of Tradition,
who meet each day
in Farthingales at pigeon
feeding time to lunch
by the gazebo,
to warble the music
and wimple their spinster tales.

There's the ginger-bread throng
that's gathered by the stump
where a street-barker barks
in his fireball frenzy,
while his short stealthy partner,
his "Pick-a-Pock", garners their wage.

Then down that cockney path
they strip their make-up,
shed their wigs, toast their day

with ice cream puffs
and black cigars, and just
sit back on an old park bench,
while passersby toss pennies
at their feet, mumble prayers,
and amble on home through the evening.

This Afternoon

There seemed nothing so important now
than to stand silently at the snack bar,
dim, without lights, and watch the care
with which the frail old woman
guided each small spoonful
to her mouth, painstakingly, slowly,
through each suspended motion,
with each suspended pause,
to finally look up, searching the moment
to meet my eyes
with her powerfully cherishing smile
that bade me watch a bit longer if I wished.

The Khaki-Monster Speaks

In 1978, Dr. Ivan Toms, age 25, served his compulsory
two-year tour in the South African Defense Force.
Subsequently, he served disadvantaged black people
in Crossroads, Cape Town, as the only physician
for 30,000 people. In 1987, he refused
additional SAFD conscription. On March 3, 1988,
he was sentenced to 630 days imprisonment.
In his words, "I refuse to serve in an army
that defends Apartheid, rather than the whole nation `
of South Africa."

*   *   *   *   *   *   *   *

Reply to my protest.

27 April 1988

Dear Dr. Hirsch,

The State has the responsibility to defend and protect…
the lives and possessions of all its inhabitants,
irrespective of their political or religious views.
This burden… cannot under any circumstances
be subordinated to the subjective perception
of ethical and moral views… The welfare of the majority
must be given preference over the welfare of the individual.

The role of the SA Defence Force in the townships
is that of a peace keeping force (in which the conscript)
has every opportunity to promote peace,

goodwill and the welfare of those whom he purports
to have deep friendships with...

Yours sincerely,

(unintelligible signature)

Roundup

There must hold a certain strength
in the prostitute, trundled into a van
in her nightgown-scandals
on an evening ridden
with the stench of defection,
to look up and into the handsome face
with the baby-blue cap and golden badge,
the shoes and jacket, club and stubble
of her erstwhile client,
never letting on about the precious
piece of himself he left behind.

An Evening's Fare

Squeaking into my wooden seat in the uttermost balcony,
I hear, at last, the sonorous voices of the symphony;
musicians intoned by consensus in a fugue with twenty-six parts,
each vying for space, under the baton of a translucent conductor,
riding his train through the hall at the speed of a choo-choo,
chirping now, then pushing the score to its demise.
Horns drown violins in spit. Woodwinds run off
between the tongues of tymps.
Crisis exudes a liquid thud, the cymbal,
then two measures of thunderous applause, racing in a dead heat
to the double bar with its curious little dots,
good for ten full repeats of that thunderous applause
before the claque disperses.

At the Ball

Her hair flows back
from the majesty of her masthead.
Her shoulders rise from above the pleats
in her cape. She commands the rotunda
with the clarity of a gracious lady.

Blindfolded, the fingers
of her right hand hold a scale
with platforms that balance
perfectly the equinox of the Just.

A gigolo steps from the shadows.
Captive in his grasp,
she is danced across a ballroom floor
that rings with ambition,

whirled through the flight of a waltz
past the privileged guests, grotesque,
and into the arms of her host,

clothed as a jurist,
cordial and suave, suddenly brazen,
who thrusts her into the depths of a trance
from which she may never return.

Four Figures

I

I Sometimes pretend I'm a midnight clock.
Anxious, upset, I wake myself to pant.
I empty my lungs of air.
My back arches. My toes point.
My neck turns taut, face wry,
thumbs bent across the palms of my hands.

I grope for the paper bag by my bed,
pucker my lips and breathe deeply, slowly.
My spasms subside.

I miss Marcel. He wanted to love me very much.

II

I slice hot peppers. My fingers tremble.
I touch my eye— white pain. It travels
lightning speed in flames through my orbits,
along the tracts that swerve around my head
to implode the back of my brain,
sending me forward in jolts. I come to rest
in a humor of tears.

III

My doll sits on the pillow on my bed. I tilt her head.
She cries. I ask her why. She tells me
that since I was young
she's craved to rid me of delusions.

Well, some people die in their crystalline caves.
Some will have learned to die before crying.
Others dare not die at all. They taste a slice of eternity
before they leave. In all likelihood, I'll mourn.
I'll dangle my pettiness to help me survive.

I douse the lights and tilt her head back into place
where it belongs. Enraged, she shouts and swears
and carries on. I dare not tilt her head again,
but cover her mouth with soundproof moths
and hurry her to sleep.

IV

*Nature is beneficent. Verdant life dazzles the eye
from spring to autumn,* says he.

These words fall hard upon my aesthetics.
There are no beginnings or endings, says I.

Squirrels and oak trees seem not bothered by this fact.
Their lives don't travel beyond their nuts, says he.

But, says I, *we discovered the microscope,*
harnessed light. Now we must pay the price

by admiring all the more what we could not have seen
in the whole loaf of years that had passed us by—

He says we must be patient. We must be still.
Somehow, the rhythms will turn right
and we will smile again.

Ms. Bovich

You enter a room divided.
One half asks what you're saying;
the second, what you mean to say.
A third half asks you
what you feel when you speak.
The fourth is filled with burdens.

I trudged through the snow
up a long flight of steps
to a hovel, to see a frail old woman
huddling—with the odor
of cancer everywhere.

*Death plunges through open windows
and doorways in search of fragile women,*

I found her couch, batting shredded,
carpet wrung to its mat by muddy shoes
trenched from the kitchen
up the stairs, as if to a spire
with a cross against the sky.

*laughing at their helplessness
thirsting for their bile,*

She sat in her housecoat,
thin black hair, rhomboid face,
sunken cheeks, cursing the seasons,
stumbling on her words.

doting on the frailty
of their strands of fading hope,

Tears leaked from behind her smile.
Each of my soothing words
seemed but another blow,
pounding red hot ingots into fear.

stalking through the miserable night,
standing on the empty corners
of every street, shivering without a life
to wrap around his body to give him warmth,
patiently waiting for prey.

In the end, she sank back in her chair,
exhausted.
She rose, smiled, and led me to the door.
She took my arm.
Hesitatingly she whispered,

Doctor, goodbye.
Will you marry me?
We both knew what she meant.

The Crowd

Have you ever raised a banner
that bled its way to half its mast
where it lived in effigy
for the rest of its life?

Have you seen a drop of water
in a rapid stream
buffeted from one rock to the next,
bruised and battered
by the stinging epithets of a crowd,
teased and coaxed by swimmers
that have gathered
to see the drop disperse and drown
in its wake?

Parts of Me

The boundaries of sorrow
and torment are thin,
tragedy and anguish, slim.
They race chaotically
through my mind.

Parts of me cheer. Parts revel,
laughing while I grieve.

Some parts barely rise
above the insufferable
while others grow rich
on the serendipity
that brought me into being.

Most secrets are not seen
in spoken words,
but parceled into slices
wrapped in skin and bones,
hung in booms of silence,
lost in pools of acid rain,
killed by useless afterthoughts.

And I roam in a circle
of ghastly friends
who have no inkling
of my presence at all.

Intuit

Hearts erupt.
They give us voices,
eyes and ears,
touch and sight,
warm our organs of love.

They tap our vats
of steel and taffy,

swirling us in and out

from under bridges of daring,
adventure and cause:

Cause. Messenger of life,
strummed over and over again.
Passions stripped
of their pants and shirts,
blouses and skirts,
bounding silent rhythms
through the tyranny of doubt.

Doubt floods a thirsty season!
Thirst? We reach for our better lives.

Epiphany

If I told you I tumbled
headlong into odes, hymns,
dialogues, dissertations,
precisely those into which
I'd buried my flaws
under crusts of awkward claims
and childlike fables,

if I told you I turned
my flaws to a woman,
the timbre of her voice,
the features in her face,

that we found
the super-conscious
parts of ourselves
in silken threads
sewn to our organs of love,

if I told you that white
was the color
of my true love's hair,
that she lives in her portrait
by the side of my bed,
that her smile
sweeps the room
while I sleep.

Stara Majko, Mila Majko, Moja Draga Majko

Old Mother, Gentle Mother, My Dear Mother (Serbo-Croatian)

I came upon her in her room,
weeping to a portrait of her son.
I asked her softly,
Stara Majko, why do you weep
to that portrait of your son?

Because he has left me, pleading,

    make me a bag. I am going
    to the hills where the forest
    will fold itself around my heart.
    And in my arms, I will carry my rifle.
    It will sing through the trees
    and soothe my torment.

I came upon her in a ravaged field,
weeping to the grave of her son.
I asked softly,

Stara Majko, why do you weep
to the grave of your son?

She kneeled and spoke to the wreath
on his stone,

My morning star,
          my golden light in the heavens,
you will shine like the radiant bloom of a flower
until time claims us both no more.

Her tears wet the ground. They swelled
in small pools. They fed the thirsty brush.

In a slow deep voice, I asked,

Stara Majko, Mila Majko, Moja Draga Majko
Why do you weep for the soul of your son?

She cleared a space beside him.
The earth disrobed before us.
She lay in her mourning raiment
The loam closed around them both
and the grass folded back into place.

The Song of the Watchman

Der Wächterlied

Night splits the valley,
swallowing whole
the lives of its folk.

For we who remain,
time shrinks
to white linen hopes,
knotted end to end
as a sign
of surrender to the Styx,
on the rim
of the pit of Hell.

In my trivial world,
a watchman raises
his lantern to uncover
a whore. A soldier
urinates in vapor trails
against a wall.

Frightened, the whore
reaches out to die
for loss of her beauty.
The soldier packs his rifle
and crawls
through the trenches
that furrow his world.

The watchman sings.
He lights a passage
in the fissures of Earth
for those who yearn to rise,
who have lost heir need
to purge themselves,
who are willing
to smile in the shapes
of their disfigurement.

On the Magnificence of Händel

What defines creation?
The sorrows we've seen?
Speechless tongues that fold
in their slackened shadows?
Lips turned black;
not ashen, but pitch?
Conjunctions of the moon and sun
in our houses of opulent fortune?
Shouts of trumpets? Cymbals?
Odes and hymns
to the irrepressible deity
who seems to sanction
our hate and our murder?

Now the choir grows faint, then still,
then suddenly sprouts in profusion.

I hear a million—one or two or twenty two
or three cadences reach up, one by one,
to fill us with light and fresh bread.

If I told you that Händel had placed his Credo
in the palms of our hands, could you glean
the immensity of this night?
Would you care?

Granny

Her thoughts congeal.
They shrivel down her right arm
and into her lap—
only grannies know
the real price of a crown.

You paint your portrait large
with many layers of caked cheese-oil,
your portrait small, by gumming it
with gouache in flourishing headlines.

You make small statues large
by conquering twenty villages,
large statues small,
by crunching them
into the pocket of your vest
to carry home for dinner.

When doctrines fester
and colonies crumble,
grind to sawdust
in the cold cold ground,

then only a crippled granny
with deep set eyes
and bulbous knuckles,
only a feisty granny,
will survive the assault.

Animal Crackers

with a picture of caged animals
in a circus on the box

On that cardboard box
stained red with yellow glitter,

salaam to sick-li-ness!
Pick the picture. Twine your brows
to your likenesses in neon glow—

Milords and Ladies-like, a toast!
A flourish and a low bow
to your elegant crests and tresses,
petty-greed swashed in lucre stuff,
to your manly-lady spats and gowns,
strutting proudly
through those caged panels,
flaunting, trotting up and down
your mendacious coups.

Animal Crackers!
Braised in decorum!

Pompity haute cuisine!
Now parade through the morsels
(the mortals) themselves.
Stalk each others' species.
Feed fine upon your baked mates.
Drop the weak ones. Wine for toast.

Scheme in your panty-caked silence,
waste in the water of your soup.
Crouch in your tight-lipped box,
your light-tipped pox,

so piquantly cherished,
so perished,
so posthumously spun
into mourning,
with the bite of the Bereft.
All gone.

Two Discoveries

I

I folded my arms
into the warmth of your body,
hid my eyes from their sight,
searched all the tenets I could find
to feel my mettle.

We swam against the currents,
inflamed, in games of climax.
We fell to sleep together.

I walk uphill, a champion,
a hero in a gallery of heroes,
with admiration for your power
to forge my life,
for the penny you placed
in my right hand coat pocket
to pay for my passage.

II

Could it be that shale turns
from red to brown
in the hollows of sleep,
that trees shed tears
at life's end,

that elegance endures,
like a candle,
wakened by the beauty
of its flickering light?

Could it be that a desert
bears fruit and a picture door
swings wide to a garden
in which we meet our child once more,
and the seventh wonder
of her Morpheus' world?

Gargoyles

Gargoyles promenade
across the weathered whiles,
juggling ugliness
with innocence,
scowling joy and fear
upon the suppliants below.

From mystic chapels,
from the chancel
down along the nave,
noble monks soothe
their fiducial maladies of faith

while hunchbacks swing
from rafters on ropes
strung from belfries,
chiming life through the air,
nurturing sacrificial loves
found only in great books,
those burned on the pyres
of judgment and creed.

Listening with the Third Ear

The way we think is by spinning silk
into threads----chenille, blue on blue,
sewn into a day that has never
felt as beautiful as this before.

We think in nuances, inflections,
mauves and fuchsias that merge
into images in modules of time,
in images, dreams that surround us.

We bathe in thoughts
that loop our impulses
up from their *depths,*
through our *middle-minds*
(that search and decode them),
to *awareness*, with useful ways
to pronounce ourselves to each other,

like spoonsful of rain that add inches
to a flowering bud, lifting it higher,
more lucid than ever it had dreamt
of being before.

We listen with our third ears to silence
and dissonance, random tonalities,
echoes of chance that thrive
inside the vital lives of each of those
who hold us dear—who give us our majesty.

A Source of Life

How could I know?
Through dilated pupils,
life seems large and vague,
not yet born.

In a quilted night sky,
large shrinks to small enough
for me to touch the memory
of those who have come before.

But landscapes intervene.
So many,
swimming through my peace,
I think that only from longing
can I reach beyond them,
to capture the instant, a scintilla
sufficient to understand who I am.

Your features, immense, subdued,
fly by, firing my sight,
exciting my senses,
spinning into seismic morsels
that challenge the depth
of my thought. If I fail you,
the instant passes and gone
is my power as a source of life.

I Rust in Thick Cream

I rust in thick cream without meaning,
like a skeleton without bones
or a slab of stale bread
in a bin where it cannot live or die,
only mildew and rot.

Each night, I fly
through a sky of thunderheads,
riding the exhilaration of fright,
fleeing some delusional monster
while submitting to its rage.

Then Sometimes I sprout
from the words I fear most.

I burst into language,
search for a credo in which to believe,
or rust without meaning,
like mildew in a muddy spring.
Alone.

This Year

was very bad.
Its impoverished limbs
bled the sky, drawing down
all its grey rolling substance
of thunder; steel hammers,
that pound and forge
red ingots of the Earth.

Rain boiled,
caught the face
of the planet
between its muck
and the mantle below,
to disfigure its features.

Soaked and drowning,
the land retched violently.
The torrid Earth crumbled.

Rivers swelled and burst,
overran their beds,
devouring fiends and foes alike,
surging me to the nightlife
of the sea.

Posthumous

Death must be the skeleton of Time,
young and well figured like a Hero or a Venus,
like a Faust pressed between two covers of a book,
as on the left, the remains of shriveled age,
as on the right of the page, youth.
Notwithstanding the lengths of their lives,
do they not both breathe? Are they not the same?

Do they not shape legends from the humors
in their eyes? Do they not merge
in a posthumous "Family of Man"?
Is there no suitable dialectic for their lives?

Time bends the night in waves across the sky.
Gravity is but a state of mind
dropped to Earth for the blending
of disparate wonders
that burst with serendipitous pulses of light.
Is swagger not rhetorical?

I was not born to be suckled in my dotage
by an Angel of Death, an infertile cherub
of granite, by companions, by children or spouses,
their versions of Deus Irae, by words and dances
sung in curls of smoke that stain my cathedral
that dwindles to embers in a life
that was never fully lived at all.

I've reproduced my image in a mirror
rather than in the eyes of a child.
I feel myself reduced to doddering,
with the coming of the crystalline frost
that leaves my stinking parts
a fleece of frozen wishes.

I've traveled faster in kilometers than in miles,
grown weightier in stones than in pounds.
In time, that leaves me with my having died.
Then what shall I see? What will I find my image to be?
Will my dissolution make me cringe or strong?
Does dissection hurt?

All

Dear Mother of Beings,

ALL must be round and infinitely large,
   a circle or a sphere without end,
     loping back upon itself
        to orbit its meager beginnings.

Souls sought words before they cried for time and space.
   Words hatched symbols for twilight and dawn,
     driving us to pause, to copulate within our minds,
        to sprout stories like vineyards that flavor our wine.

The horizon is perfectly straight, bounding into the future
   to form new dimensions,
     racing blindly to their own demise.

All swashes our linear sky with conflicts.
   We build mountains of crystalline snow,
     mark our depths with buoys that hide emotions,
        rigid, right, aliens, hostile to the humors in ourselves.
        Yet sometimes we think we are glad.

Good Day

Brilliant anthems
streak the sky,
filling streets,
driving girls and boys,
honky-tonk dudes
into the arms of their lovers,
hearts into crowded subways.

Out from under the sign
of the Pawn Broker's Guild,
patriots perch on galloping studs.

Hail to guardians of that certain
type of freedom reserved for the mob.
Hail.

Toccata and Fugue

The sun set beyond the rim of the Earth.
We walked along the path
amidst the stones, between the cypress
and the rusted picket fence,
past the graveyard, up the steps,
and through the great oak door,
into the massive cathedral,
home of our creeds,
where sacred illusions
summon our awe.

Fright and Pity spread their tales
across the tapestries that draped
the narthex walls.
Lavender banners hung from trumpets.
Princes flaunted their armor, lances, shields, stallions.
Misery cut the air with tempests and plagues,
with wrath and tears and agonal cries
of the penitent while the pulpit stood above us,
proud and priestly, gaunt and bare.

Ich Hatte Viel Bekümmernis. *

A toccata appeared in overwhelming tones
across the face of our silence,
speeding its chaos into scarlet-sounding ribbons
with the clarity of truth.

Suddenly a trill appeared, solitary, slight and frail,
completely alone, lonely, yielding to one,
two sketches of three sparse chords
befitting the stroke of a Master.

The organ struck with a ferocious force
that gripped the nave in terror.
Bolts of cacophony pierced the rearmost pews
of tattered wretches, girded only
by the tender ways with which they sing
their dead to sleep:

Sei nun wieder zufrieden.**

Theme over theme, beneath theme
ground ranks of pipes into festering
slashes of sound—

I flee.
The world I flee—

To flee and wander—
To wander the temples—
Which temples? What arks?
.....What ark holds the Question
so long and so deep, it can never end?

Time came to become a fugue,
to capture the dignity of a fugue,
dauntless, haughty, scheming,
off to sniff the keys, to meddle
in the music that brought it to life.

A fugue assaults, slithers,
hurtles shocks of quakes to the zenith
where martyrs sing their Sabbath,
thrusting tidal waves of sound
down granite pillars,
inspiring awe, hope and forgiveness
throughout the great hall.

Psalms grew weary, quarreled and fretted,
pausing on the ledges of sonnets,
sinking their missives to sleep.

In the silence that followed,

faith scaled the ramparts.
Suppliants rose to claim, each,
his share of redemption.

We turned to the aisle, through the great oak door,
past the picket fence, down the flagstone path
studded with graves, under a frozen moon,
almost round, almost green, hanging from its orbit,
a smudge on a portrait of stars
that teetered on the brink of creation.

* *Ich hatte viel bekumernis -I Suffered Greatly*
** Sei nun wieder zufriede— Come again and be rested O my spirit
Cantata #101, J.S. Bach

Opaque

I drift from one place to the next.
from one month to a year
along one path then another.

I hear a voice and wonder
if it ever laughed,
when it was born,
who was its mother,
where it has traveled,
what colors and shapes
have been sewn
into its state of mind.

My eyes are burning.
Fugitive visions spin,
too many cross my nights.

Lenses are for writing shorthand
what you want your mind to see.
Lids, like erasers, sweep across events
you need to hide,
reflexively whisking them
to the back of your brain,
to store, to love, to scold,
to murder, to mourn,
and walk away.

Sometimes I wish
I could remember your name.

Often, I've wanted to touch you.
Once in a while I cry just a bit.
I hide my tears in my pockets
so no one will notice my sorrow.
I hide in my inner world, alone,

where isolation, like the blade
of a samurai,
cuts in all dimensions at once,
paring me down till I beg
for the slightest sign of death.

Morning Walk

Look low
across that field.
See the sun
stream from the body,
from the shoulders
of that barefoot child,
foraging, ceaselessly,
scouring the brier and the weeds,

> *imagine the call*
> *of an emerald bird*
> *for her mate,*
> *searching an empty dawn,*

where no sound
can be heard
but the rhythmic swish
of the young one,
barely a woman,
scything the wind,
on this dulcet morning
that illuminates the face.

On the Fifth Page

The way I look
into your eyes,
the words on their pages—

the first four,
read again and again,
reveal your struggle
with the many shapes of life.

On the fifth page,
in an instant,
through an insignificant flaw
in the lens of your right eye,
a fault in the iris in the left,
I find your need to exist.

With a vital force
from the farthest star,
Earth and sky are made
to wrench apart so you might live
in peace between them.

Small Boy with Bird

A small boy in an oversized coat
and sandals hid behind a bush.

Ten soldiers crossed the courtyard
in flawless rows of leather and steel.

The wall beyond was chipped
where some had aimed to miss.

Naming each finger on each trigger
of each rifle, slowly, one by one,

he knew which bullets would score
and which would not.

On the final command,
he flicked open the latch
of his bamboo cage
and lost himself
in the glare of the sun.

The Bridge

There in the snow,
lies the silhouette of my son.

From over that bridge,
Night came to stalk our streets,
to split our valley into bits,
to swallow whole the bodies
of the sleeping.

Our school still stands,
a proverb, vacant,
frozen in time by the merciless slice
of a sintered wind.

My son still plays in the snow
on the ground where his silhouette lies.

Each morning I cross the bridge
to the end of the Earth.
Each evening at dusk, he takes my hand
and leads me home.

Sometimes he is hungry. I watch him
rifle the cupboard for something to eat.
Sometimes he has died.

Silhouette of an Angry Owl

Dawn unfolds the eastern sky
to the dint of marching boots.

Our flag ascends its pole,
quivering as it winds
through the rain.

A bugle sounds in the distance;
mountains shorn, rivers,
torrents rushing red.

Evening detonates the western sky.
Our wounded flag descends.
My boots chew holes in my feet.
I stumble through clotted bogs,
through meadows, headlands,
to trench myself in a bit of sleep.

Midnight spawns the silhouette
of an angry owl
perched on the silhouette
of the bough of a lifeless tree.

Devotion

I've seen slogans rich with bravery,
scattered with rape.

Each day we scorched a village.
I shot a child, with only dibs of doubt
and my shiny badge of courage.

For many years, I've killed my mind
against the pink clay tile
of my bathroom wall,
hung myself in the glaze
of my mirror, crushed my soul
against my pillow,
bought new clothes each day,
to keep myself from suffering.

Each night, I turn
into marble and bronze
with tributes
engraved on my pedestal,
fresh, each morning,
waking to plaudits, cheers,
to a kind of rancid glory that clings
like glue to a bird-shat-on statue,
one that cries phantom tears
in private, on a knoll in the park,
for simply doing
what he was commanded to do—
go home filled with sorrow,
confusion, regret, and devotion
for those that never returned.

Poor Birds

will vault across the Southern sky
eclipsing, blanketing

the horizon. You'll tell the world to turn
dark.

But I'll spring to life and countermand your
order.

I'll wash the streets with white ink, rags filled with
missals

you're not likely to want to read. So I'll
tell you which ones I like best, and you must

agree. But no. You'll march to the banners'
gleaming with proof through the night.

Poor birds

won't garnish the countryside. Nor shall they
sing again.

Dead birds.

You'll twitch when you've spent your
bomb, your fool's wealth spread over the
gutters, through walkways, alleys, trenches of
ravaged cities you'll never see again.

You'll actually want to go mad when
leaves turn to dust, when
trees have vanished and acid rain has
wiped itself on the setting sun.

You'll opine.
You'll touch yourself, stranger to your
soul, and opine. Then I'll remind you,

Poor birds.

And you'll strive so very hard to want to agree.

To the Island of Skies

My child fell in with a cadre
of angry eagles
with tawny beaks,
clutching arrows and flags
in their claws.

They trained him
to be brave enough
to grasp their art of bravery,
their courage to kill,
their revel in triumph.

He pledged himself to the ranks
of the corps, learned their jingo,
slayed their Jinns.

He marched. Endured. He followed
the heartbeat of drums and taps,
purple hearts, deafening rounds
and raptures of death,
to live forever on the Island of Skies.

Cast in bronze, how hard it is
to turn one's zeal to tenderness,
carnage to kindness,
each day, to walk
through the heavens, unafraid.

Aftermath

Who remembers the homes,
tile roofs, cornices, portals, doorways,
of those that lie below?

Laurels bloom by the Eastern wall
to soothe the salacious Monster of Havoc.

Perhaps he rages when he's cold.
Perhaps we die when he thinks of death,
melting gold to lead,
when his plagues spill their blight
on the deep red fields of the peasants.

I've returned to a village
that may never speak again,

to a house of disjointed skeletons—
to my father's stern resolve,
my mother's care,
to their gravestones;
to specters that suffer their stories
each night, that live in blood
on the doorposts of God.

Massada

I live in a room with no ceiling,
no space or time,

with no walls or windows,
in a city that bathes in its ruins.

I walk with no floor beneath me,
see without vision through a history
flush with manuals for grieving,
for those who loved, were saddened,
empty, insufficient, guilty, with rage.

I've drowned in saltpeter,
narcotized by slogans,
dependent on food served in baskets
of rituals and allegories
molded into medals
I tried so hard to deserve,
and comrades who perished,
so many times, once more
in my arms.

My Room

Hunger takes the last
of us to bed.

Sunset covers the ground.
A dead bird recalls
the creation of wings.

Men grasp their frailach
tight in their circle of arms.
Infants steep in the last
of their mothers' milk.

You must dress
your brightest
to watch for His loom,
your clothing spun and woven
in the rain of the onslaught,
at the gate of His temple,
in your Book of Life.

,

What I Learned from Years Abroad

Have you never felt
the nightmare's touch
of a frozen hand, the threat
of strangling beads of sweat,
of vows damned
by kisses trickling
promise into your right ear,
bleeding out your left
when you were full of sleep?

Which part of you has not danced
with whoring pomp bathed in rain?

We dip only once in the earthly
stream, bloom only once
in sky-light, swill only once
the lousy brew from a smelly cask
of rotten grain.

In the end, I might follow
the Master once, or once again
in another age, another shape,
with another kind of troubled whelp,
or simply forfeit my turn,
limp as thistle under mulch
that feeds the shallow sod.

But then,
I sometimes think

that a well earned death
bears that kind of dark
from which blueberries grow,
turn true, and sometimes reach
for the warmth of heaven.

In Search of Sleep

I feel like a fetish,
a coalition of chapters
of rancid books that strive,
each one, to conquer my nights.

I sleep in a forest
of stroboscopic beams
of moonlight that climb
the cliffs that line the gorges
that blanket the rivers below,
reminding me
of the nature of beauty,
that which dissolves
as I scan each page
of my troubled life.

I fly through a void that swells
into grandiose delusions
of some ideal,
viewing myself in a cavern
of soft gypsum seams
that course
through strata of stone,
glistening stalks of crystalline white
that crumble into bits of chalk,
into powder in my hand,
into the anonymity of dreams.

I've lived in a mirror
that reflects the face of a dragon
with its tendrils,
bearing incoherent truths and faiths
mixed with gorges, caverns, and delusions.
I sleep as fast as I can
to avoid slipping back into childhood.

C'est Dommage

You are nearest to yourself,
no matter what you say.

When you come to grief
and starve
to save the children,
they run away and hide.

My Seizure

Words refute each other.
Hardships ravel.
Everywhere draws near,
pruning my senses,
whipping my soul.

A gargoyle spews rain
from the dome
of a sunken cathedral,
to flood the underworld
at the nadir of its night.
A griffin lunges
from the subtle light
of a rose window
to bore through my spirit,
to swallow me whole.

I cannot move, only doubt,
shuttering, struggling
like a newborn
caught in its mother's womb
on the eve of her dearest moment.

When I wake, I'll not know
the depth of my absence.
I'll not remember
the strength of my doubts.
Only your face will meet mine.

Mood Swings

Exhilaration

Who am I,
soaring inside this cacophony—
irrational doubts and contentions
that stream across my night?

I ride the exhilaration of fright,
fleeing while submitting to its hunger
that devours me in waxen laughter
spread around the walls of my room.

I assume the stance of a king.
I reign my wooden horse
on a carousel that grinds
its tunes to smithereens.

Faster, faster, bobbing up and down,
I wield a sword in my left hand,
reaching with my right arm
to snare the classic brass ring.

I cheer like an irascible child
to the beat of a waning tune—
broken bellows, crusting valves,

a calliope slowing down to dribbles.

Crumpled rondos cover the stone
that marks my grave. I die happy!
Immensely happy, in my boundlessness.
I die into morning to finish my flight,
exhausted from my gallop to hell.

Depression

takes its costly toll—
requiems, odes, elegies,
bland, blurred,
from my bottomless sorrow,

as I strike my spine,

over my left shoulder

with a right handed switch,

rhythmically bleeding

like a penitent monk
who suffers original sin
with celibacy, with streaks of guilt,
in a trail of tears, in ritual sorrow,
yearning the blessings
that must surely come when he dies.

Misery takes one's life for a cause
that may never be known to anyone,
but the soaring and sorrow
we celebrate tonight,
is forgotten in the chorus of the day.

Eclipse

The moon collides with the sun   We are left in distress
We learn to weep   yet we dare not die
Trapped in sheets of newsprint   our shadows burn

                         to smithereens

We live in crystal parlors   We learn to drive
our flashy cars   turn to grime
drawn with ribbons   wrapped in plastic foil
across the paper face   across the face
of our planet   across our planet

                            Earth

Gulag

This is a moon that hurts—
a vengeful moon
that shears tall mountains,
burns forests to pinewood smoke,
clouds to shadows in streams of ugliness.

This is a moon that smears its light
through my bars,
down the walls of my cell
to sweep me up in its dunging claws.

Days wing by, lopsided, left to right to left

two swings forward, one swing back,
pendulums driving their minutes,
like jostling the cage of a lion or a monk.

An inmate scales the wall,
pierced by barbs, ripped by bullet-spit,

caught in rungs that carry him

to the crown on his grave.
His entrails drip bilious-green
in the morning sun.

His blood stains the muddy ground red.

I hammer, split rocks, sweat salt

till the shrill of the whistle

or the bell at the dumbing down of day.
Back in my dungeon, pretending remorse,
my mind bleaches raw, pours freely
the color of stagnant waste

drowned in slurries of sleeplessness.

The day has died on its throne.

Venus sweeps across my eyes,
filling their chambers with the force
of my longing, while our planet,
passionless, spirals the sun.

Now hear! Beware the slogans of Triumph,
for so comes the hour of great contempt.
Zarathustra, prophet of vengeance,
reigns in his Tempel seiner Lebenswelt.
His troops storm the courtyard
in brutal black boots, with bullwhips,
to maul, to pick the pockets
of the faltering dead, the cajoled,
the blind, paltry beggars
who plead for their bread,
all drowned in the soup of submission.

And so, my friend, you must cling
to your struggle and find your own trust—

For strange is not strange. Truths can estrange
by the order with which they bring order.
Despots, bursting the rebars buried inside us
to shatter the concrete limbs of our lives.

    To love, you must find your tender home in the sky.

For tenderness lives in the grasp of wonder

that soars through the heavens in search of its wine.

.

One can grieve for what has been left behind,
but cannot leave himself behind
to grieve the loss of his future.

Now the moon goes mad. She twitches.
She thrusts her tides, wrenches them back,
sucking sand, taking lives in her riptides.

My memories melt in the ink I used to use,

invisible words on pages of shreds.

My voice rises from the woodwork to remind me:

      You walk the path of martyrs,
      ordained to follow stoutly on.

I visit the wall of barbs,

green shadows on red morning mud;

the pendulum rusted, minutes smirking,
known all the while I would walk alone,
beginning my death.

I don the robe of a dirge,

march through tyrannous doctrines
to the center of the city.
The clock on the tower devours its faceless days.

I follow my footsteps to the scaffold,
slowly up:

> one to three,
> four to six,
> seven to nine,
> to ten.

Sealed in a hood that obscures my existence,

I affirm my faith in my countrymen.

A hangman is hired to laugh to the finish
and swallow the blame. Hedging, reluctant,
glove on the switch, with a single thrust,

he'll walk home to his prayers,
to fitful dreams through silent nights.

I feel the noose that shatters the day,
the instant that drops one's shoes,
his pants, his shirt, and the beating of his heart

through a hole in a pinewood floor,
with the crick of his lifeless goodbye.

The trap door will open, snapping me down
like a herring into the mouth of a shark.

I'll drop. Quiver. Convulse.

I'll leap through claps of thunder, flashes of clarity,
cavernous grief, to the twentieth ceiling of the sky,

once there, to dissolve in the rheum of my planet,
to sing myself to dust.

Bombs

Childhood held each night in its arms.
Each evening you appeared in perfusion,
borne warmly by each mirror in each room.

Windows blew out, curtains shredded.
Thunderclaps glazed our stones and streams.

I carved your name on the splintered bridge,
the rotting bench in our garden.
I wrote your name on your grave with care
to protect the past from oblivion.

I lit fluent lamps of language
in crashing bursts of rage
that burned the sky to fossil,
to gall and grief.

I see your smile on each building.
But we are evanescent and our passions
caught by the wind and carried
to the corner of our room
where we'd played wooden soldiers,
where childhood held each night in its arms,
each splintered grave and its tryst with Oblivion.

Blood Moon

Her hand formed a ring
around the flame of a candle.
Her vision unfolded.

She whispered the vow
she lay on the water
in a marble dish,
where it mingled with faith.

She pressed her fingers
onto the frets of her lute,
spinning sorrow, contrition.

Orange flame wound
into a spiral of smoke.
Sins faded from the folds
in her habit.
Her mission unraveled,
Lady of the Lake.

Sensibility

I

The ultimate mark of children
lies in the way they permit themselves
to love;
where collusions are welcome,
amusing, good-natured scrawls.

They bathe in clouds
that tweak the polar caps of design.
For them, the skyline merges
the future with the past,
disjoins the biased from the just.

Children are the birth of a concept;
the joinder of dovetailed planks
of play that create remarkability.

II

I gaze through my prism
that hangs in the morning sun.
Inflections roll back and forth
across my bedroom.
Spectra mingle.

Clusters of children
own each other's pranks

by rites and codes,
by strengths of their senses,
by their incandescence.

When I gaze out the window,
I see many colors
through the face of my prism
as it swings past my eyes
and disappears.

In my early years,

hardships found their visions
at night;
its sinister moods and manners,
its whispers,
in its totems and rituals
dissolved in questions,
in conflicts that mocked
the value of life, itself.

I've dreamed of children
streaming from homes,
from cities,
from fires that gorged
on trees and wildlife,
while our sun boorishly
marched across the sky,
turned its back,
and sank into darkness.

I view my mother and father as fiefs,
held subject to their futures
and their pasts and the lengths
of their tedious lives.

And I ask myself *why do I write*?
To change the tilt of the Earth?
To view travail in a novel way,
in some philosophical way,
out of fear and distrust

and the fright of helplessness?
to stave off the night?

Must I still have to learn
that the reader and poet are often one,
with the same extraordinary lives
we so diligently work to retrieve?

When the Journey Was Nearly Finished,

I realized that the main thing
for me was to exist.

I'd entered a forest, cut a path
through the fern and mint,
until I came to a stream.

I bent to drink. As I was filling,
I slowly melted into water.

I flowed into a river,
plunged over rocks, drifted to sea.

I followed a ship
that followed a solar wind
to where the twilight
met the morning sun.

With the marriage of space and time,
end with beginning,
my trip was no more. The ship sank
in the pitch-black center
of our galaxy.
I was sucked through an infinite hole,
and never woke again.

.

On the Hourglass of Existence

I

The slightest moment counts thirty seconds,
and others follow suit. Seven flaming wicks
melt in a fresco of fear and adulation.
Four sluggards down their gin in a game of craps.
Twelve cherubs squeak.
Each prays to the end of the year
when they fall into a pail of soapy wash.

II

Men and women and their ancestors cry out.
Horsemen wreak havoc struggling with Doom.

In an avalanche of years, children play.
They dedicate themselves to their fullest,
the sort that kneads their grain
and works their twists of boundlessness.

III

Its wings, head, palpating heart, tentative eye,
impoverished, yet elegant, a point of view,
an artist attempts
to paint a meaningful purpose
that will rise from the canvas

to infuse our sensibilities to celebrate
his posthumous accomplishment.

IV

In the sequence of birth and death,
I see myself with questions
on the nature of perpetuity,
the extradition of time.
Answers of the day swallow me each night,
when answers are the last things I need;
but peace, the first sign of immortality
of the most endearing kind.

Humility

I've striven for paths to happen.
I've searched my spirit,
repeated my name over and over again
to discover whom I want to be,
or could have become, or what
I would need to earn a god.

I've had my fame, fables, adulation,
my masturbation, an infant with an obelisk,
one, two, three pangs of success.

Now freed from the accolade engines,
let me crack my cage of isolation
and watch while you flourish,
while you spin creation,
build archives, press the keys
that rinse us clean each day.

You've not yet settled on a venue for death
or determined your terms of détente.
Eventually, they will follow the lengths
of the waves in your rainbow.

Meanwhile, one day, you'll pause.
You'll wonder.
You'll learn it is you who own
your share of humility.

But this is the age of the explicit.
You must help me find the word
from your text, the word that Hubris missed
at the peak of his glory,
the word that speaks to pain of great loss,
the last word I'll be driven to pronounce,
to build, derive, to sew, stitch by stitch,
stroke by stroke, rung by rung,
from the delicate strands of words
you hold in the palm of your hand.

Your House

If you cut the wings of a butterfly
so it cries for its home
when the weather turns cold,
your neighbor will tell you
your house has burned down.

What will you do with your wings?
Fly? Powder your fingers
and leave some shit wherever you go?

I'll give you a banner. Unfurl its beauty.
Hoist it on that pole, then cut it down.

And, by god, people will see
what you've done.
You'll regret yourself.

Your neighbor will give you
a forest to love and I'll give you
back your home
on the street where you lived.
Butterflies pollinate flowers,
don't you know?
Wing south while you're frigid.

Platitudes

Ambition is both the arm
and restraint of desire.

The future provides
a time borne sufficiency
that can only vaguely
be predicted.

Projections are tenuous.
They rely on fleeting impressions
of that which do not yet exist.

We are plastic.
We respond to contingencies.

Truths are perceptions that bolster intent.
But none can ascribe to the weight
of its fact or its substance.

Pity is the mother of humiliation.
No person should have to endure
such contempt, embraced
with the courage that helps us to try.

When I meet myself on the street,
running to catch a bus to the store to shop,
how will I know who I am?
To whom will I pay the fare?
What can I afford to buy?
How can I come to my aid
when I lose my sight of perception?

Survival

Galaxies collide,
swirling through each others' space
in quantum storms, radicals, ions,
searing heat that consumes
the future of our lives.

Spectra breech our concept of light,
and time retreats to zero.

Before we turn into gaseous paint,
by God, we must create a code
that values Cohesion.

For words do not defend themselves.
Alone, they turn into commands
that fade with time. In a void,
we cannot hear our mentors speak,
only an echo of soot and circumstance.

When we can no longer claim ourselves
for a family of man.
paper joy won't save our fashions.

Nor will we silhouette our children.
There will be no *erstwhile*. We will have lied
and shriveled in a language that rots
to instants, powdery grains of curious archives
made of glue.

In the hush that followed,

Hiroshima, August 6, 1945

a suckling whimpered.
His dusky gray turned
to speckled violet patches
against his mother's breast.

Her milk flowed red
like her nettled eyes.
Her hair peeled back
as she reeled and died.

The swollen mind
of his father flamed
and burst. Great sorrow
filled his tears.
He dwindled each day
til he died.

Faults and triumphs,
veils and buttresses
from their past
gave no solace,
but dangled
like cunning pendants,
silent remembrances
strung around their necks.

We filled the river
with rice-paper boats
like little birds,
cranes bearing candles.
Floated with the current,
they torched the night sky,
foundered on the sands
of shoals, lighting the way
for ancient souls
who lived in the depths
of heaven below.

Raindrops formed
ringlets on the water.
Armies of ringlets
marched together,
mixed in each other's wake.

Clouds swelled with passion.
The river laid waste the land.

Now the Great One lies resting.
Rice-boats bring peace
to those whose souls,
whose children sing still
in silent echoes with voices
that reach for the stars.

Truths

Plausible truths disarm me.
Unyielding truths
have the power to compel.

Lapsed time was invented
as a series of scenarios, dictates,
forebodings, grapplings,
questioning the value of faith.

Static moments, ornate,
turn to plagues that creep
through the minds of each,
infecting us all.

Meaningless facts become icons
in their own defense,
no eyes or ears, no movement,
but opinions, deprived of emotion,
defined by deficits, faults, outbursts—
facts, smiling, eager to watch me succumb
to details that profess to be truths,
prayers, blind, dying at the shrine
of obliquity, alone.

Hardships

Hardships find their lives
in times of conflict.

Hope rises from eyes that see
designs, beliefs,
that live in piquant mirrors;

dashed by ranks and files
of panes of frosted windows,
glasses filled with sooty wine.

Myths gorge on lore burned to ash.
Suns drink their light and warmth,
implode to fossil cores, to mother salt,
to fiction.

Rhetoric, sheer, disfigured,
thrusts us from our contemplations
torrid instants,

tempered heat, fierce doomsdays,
thorns that surely test our regard
for our human need to survive
and belong to each other.

I live on a stage

of masks and midnights,
in states of urgent want of need
for certainty in everything
I cherish.

Unrest draws a rampant claque
of spectators to the execution
of a cherished feeling or thought,

When a gibbet refuses to choke
the pliant neck of a hope,
where a scaffold refuses to swing its noose,
when the din of a mob fills the air
with lust for the cry of a fatal plank
that fails to fall, to turn on its hinge,

unrest, with no benediction
by the bell in the tower of god
that sits on the stone town hall,
that refuses to peel,

unrest in the smile on the face of my child
who finds joy on a page of her bedtime story,
who seems to understand what the book
has to say.

Incandescence

My god stutters and I, in the middle
of a phrase, mangled by a frozen field of words,
with the mote of a riddle—I try to think.

A meadow clusters snow, crackling,
dressed in crystals fallen from heaven---,
swept against my thoughts
by the weight of the wind.
I try to understand.

Earth's wobble would boom if the frequency
of its noise matched the range of my ears.

But silence! Inaccessible to the touch,
invisible, driving me to a frenzy,
pressing me to burst with fear.

I can no longer find my throat to speak.
My dreams, stark and sweltering,
draw hounds that snarl and leap to attack,
snakes that poise to strike.

My hands hold icy-hot scripted ingots.
I am an incandescent man
who dies to be free.

On the Origin of Myths and Symbols

In the early years, hardships
found their realities

risen from tides of destruction--
distortion. Myths of deliverance

streamed through city streets,
through chronicles, ledgers,

wood-wormed glory,
in mundane acts of "faithfulness."

Flames swept through our stories,
tales gorged on lore that burned to ash.

Moons sank back to their burrows,
each night to fossils, molten salt,

to rise each next night triumphant,
having foiled oblivion.

Suns ate their lumens whole.
And we wept.

We spun ourselves to the brink
of dereliction.

Spirits of our own design
slithered through our consciousness,

sheering us, thrusting us, disfigured,
into a plasma replete with symbols,

perversely into conflicts
that will surely test
our human strength for belonging.

Bridge of Asylum

*tribute to the children held
on the Mexican border
of the USA, August, 2018*

How can I tell you of hardship,
of the rhythms of hardship,
of names of nameless people
who have fled
cauldrons of certain death
to cauldrons of deathful captivity?

I ask you to name the songs
in the soul of a tear,
their hues, their facets,
their grieving, twisted
on the tips of a bevy of arrows
in the claw of an eagle
under the gaze of a watchful eye
on the seal, in the shadow
of the God we Trust
on the face of a dollar,
splat on a walkway,
forged into links of picket fence
that line the banks of the Rio.

I ask what lives in a tear,
each drop
that drowns a family

in flourishing strokes of ink
on a celibate sheet of paper.

Let me tell you of hardship,
of those that walked here
last night from Hell,
that dangle in the knots of our edicts
with hopes that drop
through the grates of our walkways,
one by one, into the mindless river below—
broken children slept in Treblinka.

Gatekeepers polish their guns
with pomade, tendrils with kava,
mucilage stuck to their belts
that burnish their paunches with gall.
Flesh turns red at the last frontier.

I ask you the proper name of this Sphinx
who pries from a mother
the tears of her child,
dwindled to a string of human skin,
struck from the Book of Life.

Athanor*

Oil emulsions, shellac on straw stretch across the ties that carried
the rails that lumbered through your gates.
Crucibles torched the sky, millions of skies burning smog
congealed into choirs
chanting our watchwords,
martyred by the sticky fingers
of your leaden hands.

Oil emulsions, shellac on straw,stretch across the twisted rails that
carried the trains that lumbered through the gates of your mill.

Nations wandered, still wandering
in the ways of wandering stars,
blind, through the universe,
in search of their God.

Oil emulsions, shellac on straw,stretch across the twisted Earth
that carried our people
that filled your trains
that lumbered through the gates of your courtyard, herded,
to be *washed* and burned into heaven.

Shellac on straw.

* From a masterpiece by Anselm Kiefer, German, born 1945.
  Oil, acrylic emulsion, shellac, and straw on photograph,
  mounted on canvas in vast dimensions, 1983-84.

Commentary abstracted from placard
in the Toledo Museum of Art

"Athanor", in Medieval history, refers to alchemists' attempts
to transform metals into gold signifying the spiritual quest
through which the soul seeks perfection.
This work abstracts Hitler's chancellery which was the heart
of the German war effort, the headquarters for the planning
for WW II. We find it in ruins, scorched by a fire so intense,
it has burned the sky above. At the center are three gateways –
black, brooding gates that evoke the horror of the ovens of
the holocaust, the fires of which still burn in many of our minds,
There is also the alchemist's crucible. Black grid lines pointing to
the gates suggest the railroads
that transported victims to their deaths. The partly obliterated
word, "Athanor", over the gates alludes to the doors of the ovens
where millions were incinerated.

Anthem

It is sweet and honorable
to die for one's country.

Horace (65-8 BCE)

et decorum est pro missionar
patria mori. Et mori, Dulce ;
sweet brittle death in graves
with silken plumes of ashen souls—

our arrows foiled the night,
beguiling, while I palled.
Each day died exhuming light
through tinted windows

paned with foundling portraits;
blighted, lining walls,
verses blended into fugues
that plagued my grief.

Fright, remanded.
Martyrs,
shunned from hunger's guarded secrets,
teased and laid their glaze
upon the sane and simple.

Anthems spoke from the windows
of my pew (a few, but no more,
risen from the printed parchment,

fine across a sacred page),
draped with faces, spaced in rows
where the churchyard lay.
Weary men had dug their graves
for us to spend our nights in wondering.

If you take nothing from these ramblings but

primum non nocere

you will have discovered in the healer
the treasures that he finds in his art.

If you can shed the notions that snare you,
conjectures that hinder your clarity,
you will leave this hall
driven by the power of vital thought,
protected from the need to prey,
to covet joy.

Circe, daughter of Helios, transformed offenders
into lions and wolves that roamed harmlessly
around the perimeter of her dreams.

You will have conquered the urge
to alienate the purpose of faith.

Hypnos, Thanatos, sons of Night,
sleep is *no* brother to death,
no pit for despair.
And Lethe cannot vindicate
cruelty here on Earth.

We are encrusted in iron masks,
blistered, distorting ambition,

scorning defeat, suppressing
the defects that daunt us.

When oceans wash our earth,
arks will preserve our intentions,
errors will transform to fodder
that feeds our power to heal.

But, my friend,
if you crave to be loved,
worthy to serve —
it is you who will fly with the wind
onto every doorstep and podium
on every Earth that covers the sky.

You will have learned the humble words
of a great physician:
"Ask! And you shall be rewarded."

Protégé

An artist's intention:
a horizontal straight line,
its wings and head,
triangular tail.

To learn to paint
a point of view
mysterious as life, itself.
To paint a purpose
meant to be real,
an adventure into which
he is about to discover
his innovations.

Mourning Hovers

You know, when morning
hovers close to the streets,
buildings bathe in a smog
that wraps its tender arms
around us.

At noon today, the red and white,
purple hearted boys,
hardly past the age of marbles,
chests spinning slogans,
will march faithfully forward
down the street.

Their dawns will wreak of carnage.
Their evenings will erupt in rage,
in a single stroke of a headline
smothered in fire-words, fire-walls,
fire-storms, pasted to the heat of each body.

My baby smiles. He tries to make me proud.

Where I've Been?

I

I was once a boy
who marched to the cadence
of bugles and drama,
through slogans, mirages,
proud snippets of faith.

I dragged my useless leg
through the mud of a trench.
The coat of an alien hand
frightened my pain.
and wiped from me
the sweat of death.
We smiled.

They blew us to bits
on that grassy hill that day.

Each night I see that soldier,
I kill my head against the tile
of my bathroom wall.
I wash my hands in blood
from the bottom of my heart.

I want to see my mother.
Mother, mother,
where have I been evermore?

II

Bugles slammed his helpless mind.
Banners rose against the wind
to only half as high as the night before.

Terror filled the air.
Red spilled slowly down
from the very same craters,
the very same slopes
that formed the purple mud
that coursed through the veins
beneath the folds of his skin
an ugly dream ago,
when he sank his head
beneath his pillow
for fear of exploding me
with the very same parts
of scattered speech
that had marked
the death of his comrade,
whom he loved evermore.

Out of Sight

We hid in bushes, in mounds and caves,
in streams that swelled then dried,
parched in the draughts of summer
where flourishing fields once lay,
no longer green,
where slews of brilliant stars
hid each day in burrows
to avoid the burning spell of the sun.

Orphans, we melt in our overcasts.
We eat our fruit,
the bitter fruit of the dandelion tree,
and toss its seeds to the wind,
to watch them drift through the universe
that circles the world.

My Native Land,

with its benchmarks,
scrubs, and wildlife—
amongst which I've wandered,
to which I've carefully listened,

from which I've mustered ways
to reach my thoughts,

my senses and meanings,
emotions in mazes of swells

and troughs that stream
in rushes and lulls,

borne with bursts of light
that will be left for me
to understand.

Monsieur Mime

His lacquered face—
laughing eyes with milky guile.
They droop, sag purple
into the whisper-kissed
For the sweet love of God,
entombed in his throat.

He swallows, gags,
chokes back his tears,
gropes through echoing halls,
one drama to the next,
in our taunting
Theaters of the Absurd.

Tumbling through my mind,
his lips swell tight.
His pain spoils the cream
that spills on my Daily Bisque,
taupe, chocolate brown—
that saturates my brain,
strangles my laughter
in labyrinths of fizzzz.

Transfiguration

The angry rumble
of a mob in the distance
grows louder.

Rasping fingers
seize my cry
until finally I'm swallowed
by the benefice of heaven.

The mob grows louder
as the day wears on.
Each day the mob grows louder,
closer to heaven.
More holy than before.

Waiting for a Streetcar in the Rain

My mind has left me
moldered in sludge and sorrow,
drowned in a gulch

where truths drift off
to vestiges, snared,
killed by a despot of words
I've not heard before,

where gravity sinks grief
through flaws in the mantle
to the searing center of Earth,

where young ones seep starvation
from their pores
with only raw laments and pleas
to cover their bodies,

where whispers speak to whispers,
lodged between the sheets
in every night's bed,
to quell sedition.

The streetcar is coming.
I search for my fare.
The motorman grins
like a fox.
I hate this nasty weather
but I've not yet learned to die.

Tar-rant-tal-la

These times are not real. They are square
and wanting for the convictions they have lost,
tinkling at their tops with conflicts
that have ravaged their beauty.

I cheer as I weep, hate to love, care, then flee.
Wrung of beliefs, I happen in vain,
to be shredded with my people, molten into trinkets
in a paradox of laughter and fear,
erupting with the force of the furnace on the sun.

Culturally starved, I bloat. I eat my children,
pick at their flesh, change them to blobs
in a massive bleeding of souls
across the face of the Earth.

I've been to the shrine; the excoriation of wisdom,
cloister of mute waxen men.
Their textures change with the rape of each day.

And Triumph, a clown with a belly of false yellow hair.
Geometric forms of hate exude from his stomach.
His mantra, craziness. His cunning?
Over and over again,
history repeats those anguishing words—
You've left us,, dear homeland. You've died.
Tar-rant-tal-la.

Impressions in Sounds and Stresses

A swath of ether,
a wide swath of linen ether
protects me from the Droll,
the terrible magnificent Droll,
his glut, gorging hollow,
ripping holes in the underworld,
spreading a message
that reads like the poem of a magi,
gift of gold,
thrust into the hands of Good Will,
with the sign of Wrath
under which he was born.

Higher than the beam
of a streetlamp at noon,
reading a gospel of avarice,
under the reign
of a silvery streak,
stranded on the glee
of the moment,
on the precise glee
at a solemn time of passing—

a wide swath of linen ether
forges your name
on a piece of existence, in stone,
thrust in the direction of a wind.

Tjentiste, 1943

Tears welled up on the sheer
gray face of the Zelengora,
gathering, then dripping
into its furrows, reaching down
its rocky walls to soak the scrub
and the earth below,
mixing its dirt
with Sutjeska's blood.

The river gushed
through tracts
where brothers and sisters,
plunged each other
into bogs,
into mushrooms
and lichen clusters
that marked their graves.

The mountains
marched ponderously
across the fallow glens
with no mind but to live.
Palisades
held fast to their mordant,
grinding
each other's granite faces
to dust,
striking resounding blows
that shook the valleys
with the simony of death.

In the end, we picked our way
through the forest
to find our limbs and our souls.

In the end,
Sutjeska's shores rotted gray
beneath the red snow peaks
of the Zelengora.

From out of the billows,

vultures descend.
Marksmen begin their killing.
Thunder unfolds its ugly dance of death.
Sirens, alarm bells cry out. A bite of the scythe
delivered to the neck, brings a swerving head
to part from its shoulders.
Two condemned shoulders tremble now in their grave,
kindling anger and sadness. Men and women weep.

Slashing through the purple fields,
we will set fire to the sun. Then the maelstrom
will melt. Its smoldering entrails will burst in the air,
fall, scatter, then float on the sea.

They will hiss on the cresting waves,
dissolve in the foam.

My son will be born. My wife will bear me a son.
We will sing and dance and drown
in the fermented juice of the maguey.

Before the Dawn

Spangled toy dolls wept real tears,
gunned down by robots—
no words,
only threatening bugles and drums,
from bastions
built on fine-honed fear and dread,
on countless vats
of molten skins and frames
and faces of people
clothed in creeds,
papier mache collages,
heroes that burned so fiercely soft
to gray-white ash,
strewn along the pot-hole road.

I hear the vultures shriek
above the palisades,
charging the headwinds.
I hear them pitch
in synchronized waves
as they glide across the trestle,
along the gorge.
Their rapacious eyes
seem to pivot
in colors of the sun.
Their claws, stilettos,
poise to pluck
at the ravaged flesh
of the meek.

Now, fog mutes the valley.
When it rises, we will strike.
The light of day will sink
through a cleft in the ocean floor
and we will all be dead,
all but the vultures
that beat at the wind,
swooping down
through the murk,
to taste our guile
until they, too,
spasm and cease.
We will bleed the Earth.

By A Small Stream

1983
Post WWII

By a small stream, by a bridge,
by a pub in Sarajevo, the world,
one day, came to an end.

A panicked pub-keeper
rushed through his door shouting,

"Mon Dieu!
We are utterly done!"

A small yellow tram
banged and banged
its bell to make way.
When the crowd
had dispersed,
a large bronze tablet
could be seen,
embedded in the street,
in the shape of an Austrian Duke.
With the dream of peace,
a bed of poppies
must have bloomed
in Flander's Field.

We strolled from the market
across the bridge

to find the Haggadah
that had been hidden
during the war in the temple
that looked like a mosque,
no – a Schutzstaffel,
serving lager
to the brown shirt butchers
who earned their beer
trimming flesh that they hung
from the lampposts,
plowing loins in the parks.

After years of stench had passed,
bronze plaques were laid
in the streets of the city
in memory of the dead.

I met an elderly Rachel
who spoke in five tongues,
with a few remaining men,
aged, worn, survivors
who held her hand
and studied her Talmud
to remember their God.

I heard an endless
chant of names
from the endless wall
beside the winding road
up the hill.

At the top, a field
of mangled tombstones

pitched into banks
of mangled bush.

A bearded old man,
a tzadic stood alone,
searching a crippled grave.
In his mumblings,
in his rhythmic nodding
back and forth,
his vest dripped with sweat—
his black tie slashed, armband,
silhouetted against the overcast.
Tears rolled down his pitted cheeks,
in memory.

He flagged a small bus
that brimmed with children,
singing songs they must have sung
for years gone by, innocent,
riding home from school
in the evening.

1993
Siege of Sarajevo,
Bosnian war for independence

I heard cannons
that leaped from the hills.
I saw children
pick through the rubble,
through the streets,
through the stench
of bodies of those

who'd been melted
by bullets, who'd fallen
into cesspools
that feed a small stream.
Brother killed brother,
Mothers grieved.

Red ink gushed
from beneath the bridge.
The interminable flow
colored a massacre,
then a trickling peace.

I heard stifled hymns
from between the crackling salvos,
that rose from the skeletons of houses
that littered the streets,
stifled hymns on a desolate day,
through a desolate night
ruled by leaches and scarabs,
and tearful ghosts with guns.

Listening

Listening, listen closely
to the voices that enter
into the streams,
the canals, the streets
of comings and goings,
of issuances
and absorptions,
into straits and pleats
and currents,
weaving graciously,
wandering awkwardly
through burgeoning
cascades of design,
always turning back
to reframe the past.

Little Locust, Little Moth, Little Rabbit

You have come for your place
by the cottonwood tree,
little locust in the wind,
to face the Great Spirit,
to atone for your life,
little moth around the fire.

You must find your own ways
on the cliffs, through the foothills,
and, nude and fasting,
you must take your blanket
to endure, alone, the cold nights,
predators and cruel skies,
to search for your Protector
along the Milky Way.

I am not of your kind.
I do not understand.
I do not know your shaman.
I have not suffered
to become whole and pure.

I must believe you as a brother,
for those who rise
from your hallowed ground
give me peace, little rabbit
running through the tall, tall grass.

Strange

I feel to suddenly
wield a club and
pummel
the heads of
fish
in rain soaked
gutters
and all the shells
of turtles and crabs
that emerge from
our flooded walkways,

then go home for the night
to tele-view the bloody deluge
that stirs in the bottom of my heart,
and pray.

On the third day in May,

a train pulled into the station.
The town had spread a blanket
on its the bed and gone to sleep.

Thirty blindfolded children debarked,
crossed a cobbled street
to a bus with no windows.
They felt the burnished cobbles
and the slats of wooden seat.
They felt the push of their captors.

Thirty urchins, holding hands,
groped from the train to the bus
to a fortress on the hill.

The room felt silent. It smelled of children
and chimney soot
that had clouded the world.

Can you see the blind flag that waves
from the carriage at the rear of the train,
or the weeping wren
caught in the smoke at the crest of the hill?
Can you see anything at all
with your lids sewn so tight
and the lights dimmed to nothing?
Attention.

Through Lethal Space

The panes of my window
face down on a giant night of terror.

Twelve chimes on the face
of the midnight clock
scan beams of light
that slice the vitreous bodies
of two blindfolded men
who's lives have fallen
from the pock marked wall
through lethal space,
to the frozen ground below.

I hear thunder rumble
through my village.
I watch laughter
hide from each window.
Then shutters close.
People coddle
in small boxes of sleep.

Who will be next to fall
into the mouths
of the life-eating monsters
spitting their bitter herbs
into our toilets,
wiping themselves
and walking away?

Anguish

Giant clouds of Mordor
sail in like a fleet
of wounded galleons,
slowly, surely,
burrowing their way
across a jagged sky;
juggernauts limping
over mountains,
impaled, strung
on bony peaks and crags.

Trees cringe, their leaves
stark yellow, red, brown,
flashing now like silver dollars
in the sweeping rain.

Shriveled,
consumed by darkness,
they wither. They drown
in the mauve
of the countryside,
plunge to their graves
in the thicket.

How Can I Tell You of Hardship?

Breathless children, bookmarks in ledgers,
names molded into toys.

Their shirts and pants
shine in the dark, dark light.
Dark, they lie restrained
smiling in the face of vacancy
in prison playpens
that ought never to have existed.

Orphans' after-thoughts
are left along the road,
rag dolls stolen from the breasts
of mothers by hooded skeletons
with badges and scythes.

I fought for my flag. I killed a child.
Faith claimed my soul.
I lie in a monstrous crypt
too small and lovely for me to fit.
I will die forever.

So, what is in a tear?
One part damnation,
one part demise,
whipped in unguent
as like for flaking skin,

boiled to custard cookies
that make us laugh, the more fervently
frightened to die.

What is a tear but a trick
in a monkey show in a theater,
Pablum? Cereal for bogus justices,
sloshed in gravy and soup-stone
dripped on a tie around the neck?

We watch from the moon at night,
from where childhood
is a legend, dripping through rafters
of burning homes,
and loneliness is a mother
with a desperate song,
marched through the streets
of her afterlife.

The world is a spoon
and we, custards melting
in cups of ruptured spleens
only to taste our brothers and sisters,
their father who swarms as best he can,
who lost this head,
with only a body and fins
to guide him, roaming,
shouting, lonely to bed.

There is a naked pity in the house,
I tell you, an enormous pity
that roams the floors

from room to room
crushing walls and ceilings—

I tell you there must be a pity
that roams the courtyard of hell
while we look on and talk about tittles
that crawl through our beautiful land,
Land. Land. Grief, after the song is over
and the actors, sick of war,
applaud themselves for a job well done
We hear you. You are suffering
as are we.

Cried a Dangling Drop of Blood

Crushed by a cartwheel,
   cried a dangling drop of blood,
      as it dropped into a sewer
         through a river,
   to the sea.

But the spokes of the wheel carried on,
   past the corner around the marble-bush
      down by the lead-shot barn,
         where nothing grows that's fit to eat,
            fit to eat clanked the iron-cast rims
            of the red wooden cart.

The shimmering jowls of the teamster
   bounced to the plod of his dray,

and away past the bog,
   with his whip on the back
      of his red wooden horse
         in cast rims on his flight to Hell,

where my nation'd been crushed by a cartwheel,
   wept the drop of blood.

Triumph

Canons gnash, shrines in the dark,
changing dark to dark light
to lightning dark, with claps of clouds
head-on-hand-on-head
in a windowless sky, in a broth
that should never exist.
.

Children, mushrooms, after-thoughts,
dolls ripped from ragged breasts of mothers,
with no eyes to cry or close to open.

So what is in a tear?
One part pride, another damnation,
demise, gold ,
scrubbed with pomade
as if it were skin,
fleeced, down drains for sewage.

What is a tear?
A half-mast flag salutes a missal,
an impacted bowel that bursts with hubris,
ripe with grisly knells and bells of balls.

A demagogue swims in red gravy soup,
marked as a warrior for war.

But there is pity in the house.
I tell you, naked pity.

The specter roams the nights
from room to room.

The fascist roams from room to room
crushing walls and ceilings
and small boys.

I tell you there must be a sorrow
that advocates in the court of hell,
that eats the times in which we live.
Yet we cheer.

Liberty

Beneath her copper oxide coat,
a pig iron spiral staircase
carries me inside the folds
of her robe,
through her midriff,
through her face,
almost into her mind—
certainly into her majesty,
her crown,
with its windows and spikes
that transfix the salt air
blown in from the sea,
laden with gulls
that rise from the harbor
to rest for a while
on a page of the book
she holds in her hand.

About a Woman

Have you ever watched an old woman
spinning garlands from stone,
floral paths from pebbles and trees,
boughs from marble statues?

Have you seen her search for bees
and spiders, small creatures
concealed in the spongy moss
on the breasts of mountains
with underground streams
that sing their secrets?

She sits over there in the grass
gazing up a stripped bark tree
to a robin perched
among the leaves.
She folds her legs
knitting fossils into children,
donning her morning shawl to pray.

Art of the Apparent

The world will become a kingdom.
The king will become a king,
with his shock of navy blond hair,
his courtiers, ministers, jesters,
his princes, Templars, enemies, scapegoats.

A constitution must be broken,
shattered in paper bags of bogus truths.
He must form allies, hate enemies,
with armament to kill them both.

He will have claques, minions,
pacified claques, edicts,
happy claques, lethal edicts,
and the art of apparent indecision,
of slithering words,
a repertoire of distractions,
blaming and dire fear.

Hello, I'm Fine

Words enter my ears and eyes.
They swirl through my mind.
They lodge in my lungs,
pour out my mouth,
fly through thin air
at the speed of ultrasound,
to all the crannies in the room.

Others gasp at my words,
process them and fire back.
I agree. I always agree a bit,
which disrupts the thought streams
of my friends.

Windbags burst with supercilious comments
culled from false assumptions,
surmises, imagined
splotches of mucus that mix
in the profundity of dearth.

Windlasses hoist buckets
up from crisply parched wells,
manufacturing illusions
that match the more dismal
times of day, good times,
bad times but horribly dry times,
with successions
of meaningless tweets.

I understand that each individual
holds his own key to truth,
however that may appear,
sometimes quaintly warped
and sometimes absent,
sometimes suffering to remain alive.

Hello, I'm fine.
You must be fine, too,
or I'll export you to heaven
where you'll be glad as well.

Made in the USA
Middletown, DE
01 August 2020